The Big Book of
APPLIQUE

The Big Book of
APPLIQUE

Virginia Avery

CHARLES SCRIBNER'S SONS • NEW YORK

This book is for you

Copyright © 1978 Virginia Avery

Library of Congress Cataloging in Publication Data

Avery, Virginia.
  The big book of appliqué.

  1. Appliqué. I. Title.
TT779.A93   746.4'4   78-6547
ISBN 0-684-15623-7

1 3 5 7 9 11 13 15 19 Q / C 20 18 16 14 12 10 8 6 4 2

Printed in the United States of America

Acknowledgments

I always thought that *acknowledgments* was a namby-pamby word and I shied away from using it. Then I looked it up in the dictionary, where it is defined, "to express gratitude or obligation for. . . ." I feel much better about the word now, for I am expressing both gratitude and obligation—not the common garden variety, mind you, but deeply heartfelt. And so, many thanks forever:

—To all the talented artist-craftsmen who so generously shared their work, their time, and their talents.

—To photographers Stubby Crowe, Mary Alice Fisher, and Kim Blanchard, for their patience and cheerful dispositions. Also, thanks to the other photographers who contributed and whose credits are listed throughout these pages.

—To Jody Schnautz, Sharon Prettyman, and Stubby Crowe, who helped with sewing when I got stuck.

—To Judy Avery, whose excellent art work has raised the level of this book considerably. She is responsible for almost all the drawings—the good ones are hers.

—To Elinor Parker of Charles Scribner's Sons, who not only encouraged me in this book but gave me a free hand.

—To all my family and friends, who pushed, shoved, helped, cajoled, cheered, forced, and encouraged me to get this book together for you. It is as honest as I can make it. If you find errors, I can only hope you will regard them with the same understanding and tolerance that was accorded old-time quilt makers, who deliberately made mistakes so as not to offend heaven with man-made perfection.

Contents

The Big Book of
APPLIQUE

What is appliqué? The dictionary defines it in skeletal terms: "fastened on; one material attached by sewing . . . to another. A cutout decoration fastened to a larger piece of material." The word *appliqué* means "to lay on," and it comes from the French word *appliquer*. What understatement this definition is; how much is left unsaid! And what a challenge to all of us to clothe this word with flesh and blood!

Is appliqué art or craft? We think of craft as functional and art as purely decorative, but so many different types and kinds of handwork crisscross these areas so often that the boundary lines are diffused and often erased. A painter puts paint on canvas with a brush, and the result is called art. We put fabric on fabric with needle and thread, and it is no less art just because the medium has changed. Appliqué can be art or craft, and it can be—and is—both. It depends on what form it takes and who does it, and we should ignore the limitations set by such categories.

Appliqué has been around for a long time—so long, in fact, that no one can trace its beginnings with accuracy. It may have started when cavewoman, using a bone needle, patched her husband's leather garment with a scrap of leftover hide. References to it weave in and out of the Bible. Egyptians used appliqué to decorate their tents; it was common in India and Pakistan as well as in African tribes.

During the Crusades knights used appliqué on their flags and banners in order to tell friend from foe. Some of the techniques were perhaps refined in the Orient, but appliqué was well known and widely used throughout Europe. Lavish adornment of royal and ecclesiastical robes and trappings was as common as the more modest forms employed in everyday living.

The knowledge and pleasures of appliqué were undoubtedly brought to American shores with early settlers, but that was as far as it got for a long, long time. All time and energy were spent trying to survive those difficult years, and the gentle arts of needlework fell forgotten by the wayside.

Of course, handwork resurfaced in time—it had to, for only by creative expression do we keep balance in our lives. Most women, however, were occupied with embroidery, and most had come to the new land with treasured skeins of wool, silk, and linen. This was a flourishing period of crewel work, Jacobean designs embroidered on linen with wool thread or yarn. Unfortunately, it was difficult, sometimes impossible, to replace the initial yarn supply. The luxurious wool yarns had to be imported, and they were often too scarce or too expensive for the needlewomen who longed for them. In such circumstances appliqué reentered the scene, this time by the back door. A frustrated embroiderer, lacking the yarns to cover an area with stitches, covered it instead with a scrap of fabric. This was a homely invention, but clever and innovative, and for a long time afterward appliqué was tagged as "poor man's embroidery." Needleworkers have a bountiful and amazing harvest from this little seed; they also have a fringe benefit. Such early and fruitful effort with appliqué undoubtedly has saved us from drowning in a sea of satin stitches.

Not until the middle of the nineteenth century, however, were women able to indulge themselves in this type of needlework. For years, piecing quilts had been a popular activity; many were stunning in color and design, and all were subject to the disciplines of geometry. By now, America was growing its own cotton, flax, and wool; there was, at last, an abundance of fabric, and the quilt makers lost no time in using it. It was no accident that this period in history was known for the flowering of the American quilt, for the appliqué designs were exquisite, balanced, and detailed. Curved seams and flowing lines were the order of the day, and thus were masterpiece quilts born. These were bridal, album, or presentation quilts with elaborate and intricate designs. There were family quilts, too, usually stylized floral patterns blooming in orderly fashion, sewed with stitches so tiny that they were almost invisible. These quilts were not made to be used. They were made for display and for admiration; they were made for posterity, and because of this, many fine examples are available to us now as private collectors, museums, and historical societies share them with an admiring public.

It was too good to last. The Industrial Revolution gave birth to machines that turned the pattern of living upside down. Metal monsters spewed out thousands of identical objects in a fraction of the time it took to make one article by hand. People were overwhelmed by the precision and inevitability of manufacture, and, gradually, needleworkers, along with other craftsmen, began to be ashamed of their own handwork. From time to time, all arts and crafts suffer decline, rising and falling in popularity as economic, political, and social conditions change. Appliqué dwindled along with the rest of them, down but not out.

It took a while to discover that machines were not substitutes for handwork, that they were not creative, and that the articles they manufactured lacked the endearing individual touch of a handmade item. We accepted and recognized machines, and we needed the products. We welcomed the mass-produced articles but also realized that the whole process contributed to the decline of the individual. We also realized that no machine could ever compete or compare with those two wonderful tools—hands and eyes. What an awesome team! With them, we can tell the world how we feel, what we think. What we create with our hands is ours alone; it bears our individual and unique stamp.

We won the victory by recognizing the foe; handwork began a steady comeback, and needlework in particular entered into a new and vigorous phase. Appliqué is competing with and edging out some other forms of needlework; it offers a creative balance to the world we live in. It offers us unlimited opportunity to "make our statement." You can use needle, thread, and fabric to write a poem or a song or realize a dream. What you do with this combination is, in a way, graffiti; it says, "Look at me! I'm somebody! I'm worth something! I count!"

Appliqué holds as many challenges as rewards. It has a broad and personal appeal; it beckons. There are no limitations on either fabric or design. It is an economical and accessible craft, and most of the time it is portable—here is something you *can* take with you. You can start an adventure in appliqué with little or no sewing experience, although it helps to be familiar with some of the basic stitches. Appliqué can be done by hand, it can be done by machine, and it can be done with a combination of both. It takes many and varied forms, limited only by your imagination. This book is planned to help you develop that—to see with your inner eye and stretch your mind. This is not a pattern book. Stores and shelves are crammed with books and magazines filled with page after page of patterns and designs; copying may improve your sewing techniques, but it won't satisfy those creative impulses floating around in your head.

Use this book as a springboard. Read about appliqué in its many forms, and see what other craftswomen have made; see how old patterns and techniques can be transformed into new uses, new designs. Be willing to explore, to experiment, and don't fret because someone else is better than you are. There will always be someone better and more experienced than you, but if you practice, after a while, you'll be better than someone else. Your personal involvement in this art form will keep the creative juices flowing; the act of *doing* or creating is as important as the result. The traveler enjoys the journey as much as the arrival. Fabric art has come into its own; it is a joyful experience in a world where joy is in short supply. The threaded needle is as eloquent as the gifted tongue or pen.

Bon voyage!

2

THE EYE OF THE BEHOLDER:

Ideas and Design

Before you have a design, you must have an idea. An idea isn't exactly a tool, but it certainly is a basic necessity, a beginning, for an appliqué project—or any other project. We live in a world of ideas, but perhaps our biggest problem is identifying them. When we can train ourselves to see creatively, this will provoke a mental image, and then a design can begin to take shape.

SOURCES

1. **Nature** is the most abundant source. You encounter nature everywhere. Trees have different shapes. Leaves also have different shapes. Flowers come in every conceivable shape and size and color; so, too, do vegetables, insects, and birds. Art for centuries has been based on these things, along with mountains, animals, fish; the moon, stars, and sun. Each area of nature contains its own elements of design; what matters is your interpretation.

2. **Man-made objects.** Landscapes belong to nature, but cityscapes belong to humans. Look at towers and steeples, the shapes massed together in a city skyline. Take note of a row of houses or the clustered shops in a shopping mall. These things are outside your house or apartment, but what of the inside? Your kitchen alone is parent to many ideas—a plant on the windowsill; shelves of cans, boxes, and other containers in all different shapes and sizes. Pots and pans and cooking utensils can be an interesting grouping.

3. **Family activities and hobbies.** Even if you live alone, you're still a family, although most families include others—husbands, wives, parents, children, close friends, and pets. Think of what you do in recreational time. Are you active in sports, or do you watch them? How about picnics, or a camping trip, the ballet, or swimming? If you have children, trips to the zoo or the circus are important events. Perhaps your children have favorite toys, a favorite book, favorite things to eat, a special pet.

Most of us celebrate holidays and special occasions—birthdays, weddings, anniversaries; Christmas, Passover, Thanksgiving, the Fourth of July, and Easter. What a staggering bounty of ideas are here for the taking—the difficulty is choosing!

4. **The written word.** The Bible and Shakespeare are both lavish in imagery; craftsmen and artists have drawn on these

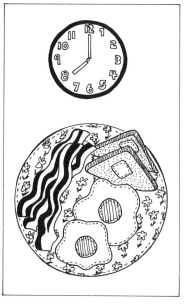

Far left: A breakfast platter offers a design; the clock above can be friend or enemy.

Left: Basic design in basic supplies.

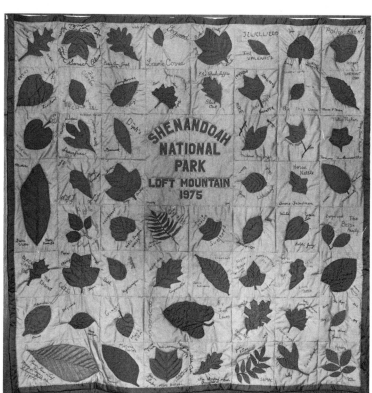

Shenandoah National Park Quilt, made by visitors to Shenandoah National Park under the supervision and coordination of Amanda Linden Moody. Designs for leaves were drawn from leaves of trees growing in the park; green appliqué on beige ground. Each leaf is identified and each block signed with outline stitching. A "nature" design at its best. Photo, courtesy National Park Service.

sources for years, yet they remain undiminished. Proverbs and nursery rhymes, folk tales and mythology, commonly used sayings and slogans are all possibilities. The appliqué hanging on page 114 is my protest against the computers that dominate our lives. I got the idea from the tiresome admonition printed on most of my bills—"Do not bend, break, spindle, or mutilate." This hanging also employs letters as an element of the design.

I've often wanted to make a fabric version of one of my favorite little poems, a poignant gem written by an Irishman, William Allingham, who died in 1889. Somehow there's been no time to do this, so I will pass the idea to you. The poem reads:

> Four ducks on a pond,
> A grass-bank beyond,
> A blue sky of spring,
> White clouds on the wing:
> What a little thing
> To remember for years—
> To remember with tears!

The idea sources listed earlier are particularly suited to pictorial appliqué; the following could be used in graphic design.

5. **Signs and symbols.** These are a part of our daily living—so much so, in fact, we take them for granted. The telephone, traffic signs, cars, clocks, and calendars are symbols of communication and transportation. The navy's language is made up of symbols, and so is Morse code. Our weather vanes are symbols, too; although they are used mostly as decoration now, their original purpose was to communicate. Thus the metal cow on top of a barn signified a dairy farm. The eagle is a symbol of America. The rooster is a symbol of Peter's denial of Christ. Our churches and synagogues are filled with symbols—geometric, disciplined shapes ready for a fabric translation.

6. **Letters and numbers.** These contain endless design possibilities; legibility is perhaps the only limitation. Both newspapers and magazines print a wide variety of these in every issue; notice the different shapes and styles. Most of the banners made for ecclesiastical processions and ceremonies are dominated by letters; so, too, are banners made for advertising purposes. Here is a little experiment in design for you. Cut a rectangle 61 cm (24 in.) by 15 cm (6 in.) out of paper. Write your name in script, keeping the letters thick and bold. Cut out the name. This is one design; look at the leftover rectangle, for here is a second design, in a positive-negative fashion. Now turn the name over, mirror-fashion; try it upside down. Each time, with each change, a new design will emerge.

7. **Other sources.** I've already covered the main areas of idea sources, and here, briefly, are a few more. Photos, greeting cards, wrapping paper and wallpaper, magazine illustrations, and ads are all worth thinking about. Use your appliqué eyes when you are looking at them.

Ethnic designs have unlimited promise. Early cave drawings, temple carvings, mud drawings and sculptured totems, masks, and ceremonial costumes are in this group. Many of them come into our culture unchanged; many others are adapted to suit our

Good-luck charms, watermarks, and alchemy symbols, from *Symbols, Signs and Signets,* by Ernst Lehner (New York, Dover).

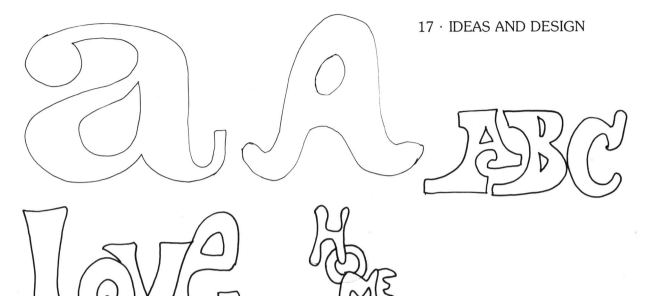

Letters shaped for easy handling in appliqué.

Note the abstract, or negative, design formed by leftover paper from the word cutout.

Ibo carved funerary stone, Nigeria.

Left: Ijo wooden mask, southern Nigeria.
Right: Carved wooden figure from the
northern Congo.
All from *African Designs from
Traditional Sources,* by Geoffrey
Williams (New York, Dover).

own time and needs. America is peopled with immigrants from all
nations, who brought their loved and familiar arts to an alien land.
These paintings, embroideries, weavings, and carvings all have
sentimental and religious significance; most could be adapted in
whole or part to a contemporary interpretation. Whether these
designs spring from Africa, Mexico, or the American Indians, they
have one thing in common: most of the shapes are bold and
simple—a very good starting point for sewn art.

America's gravestone art has received a lot of attention in
recent years; we think of it as primitive art. That is a questionable
description, but for the most part, the stone carvings are childishly
simple and most of them are church-related; thus we have angels
and seraphs and other hosts of heaven.

Keep your eyes and mind open for ideas; observe, compare,
examine, and you will be astonished at the variety of new visual
impacts. Don't trust your memory, for it has a nasty habit of
betraying you. Jot the ideas down in a notebook—and carry the

notebook with you. Keep a file with other ideas you collect—the photos, ads, pictures, and sketches. Don't paste them in a scrapbook. A simple filing system will enable you to remove idea material when it's needed and discard it when it's not.

PLANNING DESIGN

Design and fabric in appliqué work fall into the chicken-and-egg syndrome—which comes first? They take turns. Sometimes you'll have a design sharply in mind, then look for the fabric to bring it into focus. Other times you'll be captured by a length or scrap of fabric, and its color and texture will suggest ways to use it. Since it is confusing to try to discuss both design and fabric at the same time, I'll start with the former.

A design is more than a sketch or a drawing. It is a pattern, or an arrangement of ideas. Rather, it is a rearrangement of ideas. Ecclesiastes intoned mournfully, "There is nothing new under the sun." I can add, "except you make it so." Everyday objects, old subjects, and future fantasies can be combined in exciting, different ways—and you're the one to experiment with them.

Like a good recipe, design is made up of several ingredients—color, form, and balance or proportion. Let's think about color first.

1. **Color.** Color is very personal, and it is also very important. Some craftsmen have a peculiar talent in choosing effective and striking color schemes; for others, it is difficult. Color appeals basically to the emotions; it can create a mood of joy or sorrow, or convey a temperature—warm or cool. Each of us views colors differently, and we all tend to gravitate toward the ones that appeal to us. Here, however, are a few color facts that may help to shape your decisions.

Primary colors are red, yellow, and blue. These three colors are

Color wheel. Inner circle, black and white; middle area, primary colors—red, blue, and yellow; outer ring, secondary colors—purple, green, and orange. Triangles on the edge are shades from color families. Felt by G.A.F. Photo, Stubby Crowe.

Above: A human figure design. *Below:* The Eagle (Cuauhtli). From *Designs from Pre-Columbian Mexico,* by Jorge Enciso (New York, Dover).

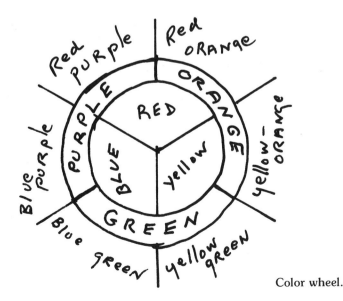

Color wheel.

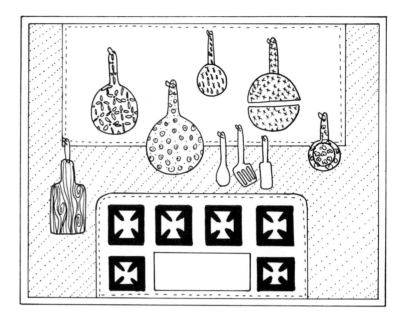

Right: Grouping of pots and pans on a pegboard creates a balanced design.

Below: Bible markers and pulpit cloth, part of a Pentecostal set designed and made by Ardis James and Wilna Lane for the Mt. Kisco Presbyterian Church. Foundation is red wool, backed with iron-on interfacing for body. Yellow and orange flames are cotton and wool in a mixture planned to reflect light. Logs are cotton velveteen. Appliqué edges were not turned under but attached by hand-buttonhole stitches. Photo, Stubby Crowe.

Right: "Le Chat" by the author. Reverse appliqué in lavender, gray, and gold with black as top layer. Color values and their importance are apparent here in the basic design, but the bird and fish in the cat's stomach are lost to view in this black-and-white photo because the color value wasn't right—a lesson to learn. Photo, Stubby Crowe.

key colors, and in one way or another, they are responsible for all the shades and gradations found in the spectrum.

Secondary colors are purple, green, and orange. Each of these colors is made by mixing two primaries—equal parts of blue and red make a true purple; equal parts of blue and yellow make a true green; equal parts of red and yellow make a true orange.

Tertiary colors are made by mixing a primary with a secondary color; the shade you get depends on the quantity and proportion of mixing. You can lighten the color by adding white, darken it by adding black. Such additions are called monochromatic, and, as you can see, there are twelve such possibilities in the color wheel. Black and white appear to the eye as colors, but actually, white is simply the presence of light and black is the absence of it.

The most visually exciting combination comes from using color opposites—those across from each other on the wheel. These opposites are called complementary colors.

Red-orange tones are warm, and blue-green tones are cool. In a design, light shades tend to advance, and dark ones recede. Colors also have meaning or significance, possibly because of long tradition. For instance, purple designates royalty; blue is the color of loyalty—remember our "true-blue" friends—and red is the color of courage, green of envy.

Value is probably the most important property of color. Value means intensity. Color value will keep some appliqué shapes in the background and bring others forward into prominence. Different hues, or shades, of the same value will look alike in a black-and-white photograph. This is a good test if you can't make a color decision; lay swatches of your selected fabrics on a white or light background and take a picture of them. Color value in such a photo will show up as dark or light and will help you choose fabrics for effect. Another test is to pin fabrics in place on a sheet, or tape them to a wall, then stand back and squint your eyes as you look. The more you work with colors, of course, the easier it will be to decide on the intensity of a shade to create the effect you want. Above all, work with colors you enjoy.

2. **Form or purpose.** What do you want to make and how will it be used? Answers to these two questions often dictate the size, methods, and fabrics to be used. A picture or hanging must be a certain size if it is to fit in a specific wall space. If your appliqué project is to be washed, you must choose fabrics and techniques that will withstand laundering.

3. **Balance or proportion.** When you work with balance for a project, you must consider not only the appliqué shapes sewed to the background fabric, but also the open areas, the ground fabric left uncovered. Having a balanced design doesn't necessarily mean it must be centered or static; it can be asymmetrical and still be interesting. This little experiment may help you in planning a design.

Cut random shapes from newspaper and place them on a flat tray or board. If most of the shapes are on one side, the effect will be a lopsided one. If most of them are above the center, the effect will be top-heavy. As you move the shapes around, you'll know whether the arrangement is pleasing or not. Perspective plays a part in this, too. It is an interesting observation that perspective, creating the illusion of depth or distance, has been developed as an American trait. Early or primitive art, whether painted or sewed, has a flat, open look, without pretense, without guile. Most tribal art is done this way, and it carries a distinct charm. Shape and color were the important things; balance and perspective did not matter. Children have this same approach, and their drawings

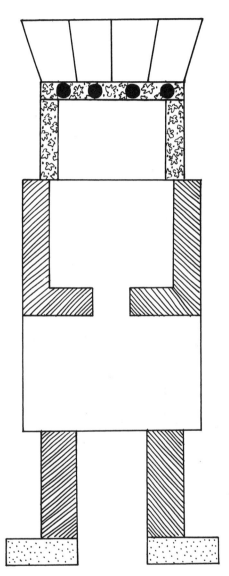

Rectangles and simple geometric shapes used for primitive-type design.

Interesting design of growing flowers arranged from triangles and rectangles.

Another design for those who "can't draw a straight line," using preformed geometric shapes.

are a delight. They have a disarming way of getting rid of clutter, of getting right to the point. It is only much later, after training, that they become aware of perspective and shapes receding or advancing. Happily, today we can choose whether or not we wish to employ this technique; it is a matter of choice.

In the section on color I mentioned that light colors advance and dark colors recede. In balance and perspective, large shapes advance or dominate, and small shapes recede. The key command to all of this, and especially for a beginner, is *simplify*. Your design will be more vigorous if it is understated. Later, you can be as complex as you like, but don't rush it. If you were just learning to cook, you wouldn't undertake a six-course dinner for your first assignment, so don't take on more than you can handle now.

When you experiment with design and arrangement of shapes, try for a linear quality, too, a rhythm that will move the eye along from one area to another. In the beginning, of course, stick to something simple—two or three elementary shapes are plenty. Appliqué a flower, a bird, the sun, a house. Line is a compelling element of design. Heavy, dark lines give the impression of strength and solidity. Right angles are strong and masculine; short, delicate lines are lively and carefree. There is a soft and feminine quality to ovals and arcs; and circles, either single or overlapping, represent the eternal mother, endless love.

Most objects can be reduced to geometric shapes—a circle, a square, a triangle. Remembering this will help you practice drawing and sketching, and this is enough for a start.

FABRICS

What a feast of fabrics we have today! Never before has there been such plenty, and never before has the choice been so difficult. Fabrics have a sensual quality; just touching them, handling them, working with them is an exciting experience.

You'll need background fabrics for appliqué work, and you'll also need fabrics for appliqué shapes and designs. Most of the time these two groups are interchangeable—it depends largely on the project. If you were making a wall hanging or picture, you could use a heavy fabric for the background; if your project is a pillow or quilt, you might prefer to use a fairly lightweight cotton. Firmly woven, light- to medium-weight fabrics are easier to use. Often the slipcover and upholstery department of your local fabric store will yield many suitable choices, which may also be less expensive than dress goods.

Wool flannel and suiting, sailcloth, duck, Mexican cotton, kettle cloth, denim, and linen are firmly woven fabrics that are easy to use. Appliqué worked on loosely woven or stretchy fabric will pucker, and goodness knows you don't want that!

There are properties in fabrics as there are in design; you can learn a lot about these properties as you work with different types of fabrics. Color and texture are the two most important ones; learn to exploit these to the fullest.

Hue means color or shade, such as red, blue, or green. The *value* of color has to do with the intensity—whether it is bright, muted, or dull, on the light side or the dark. The color of fabrics changes with texture and light. Some fabrics suggest a quiet relationship; others contrast violently. Some are exciting, others calm. Strong, sharp colors bring a design to the foreground and give it importance. Muted, grayed-down, or darkened colors give the impression of distance.

A piece of fabric may appear to be one color when viewed alone, but it will take on entirely different tones when placed against or next to other colors. Pick up a handful of swatches and study them. They take tonal quality from each other, and they also will take it from the background fabric you plan to use. The play of light on fabric also affects it, so study your work in both natural and artificial light.

3

HORN OF PLENTY:

Fabrics, Findings, and Other Essentials

Fabrics create moods—calm and peaceful, rough and turbulent. Shiny fabrics, such as satin, silk, taffeta, rayons, and some metallics, will reflect the light, whereas the dull or matte textures tend to absorb it; light shades also reflect, dark shades absorb. As there is sheen and glitter in satin and metallics, there is depth and sensuous texture in corduroy, velvet, and velour.

Felt is not a true fabric but a pressed material, and a happy choice for much appliqué work. It is easy to handle and easy to sew, and it comes in a marvelous range of colors. A heavyweight felt is excellent for backgrounds; if the project is very large you can back the felt with a piece of heavy muslin to help support the weight. Lighter-weight felt works well in appliqué designs, and it has a decided advantage in that the edges do not need to be turned under. For this reason it is a particularly good choice when working with children.

Pellon falls in this same category—another pressed material, but lighter in weight, and washable. It is used primarily as interfacing in garments, but it easily steps over the boundary line for use in needlework. Originally it came only in black and white, but now the Pellon company has brought it out in a number of colors under the tag of "Phun Phelt" and advertises it for use in appliqué and embroidery.

Two contemporary fabrics printed with African designs. The one on the left is reproduced from a mud painting; that on the right, from a bark drawing. Such fabrics are readily available today; they can be used as they are, or the shapes and designs can be cut from them and used as modern-day Broderie Perse. Photos, Stubby Crowe.

Burlap is a very popular—and inexpensive—fabric too. It is loosely woven and rather abrasive to the touch, but its coarse texture and wide range of colors have a broad appeal. It tends to stretch after a while, however, so it should be used only for articles destined for a short life span.

Plain weaves and solid neutral shades usually are more effective for use as background, since they should not dominate the appliqué design. A busy or confusing look will detract from the overall appearance. Often a small repeat fabric or a tone-on-tone can be used effectively, such as a cotton brocade or tweed.

Woven fabrics in the long run are easier to handle, since knits have a tendency to stretch. The heavier, stable double knits can be used for appliqué shapes in small sizes, and, like felt, the edges need not be turned under since they do not ravel or fray.

The question of whether natural or synthetic fabrics are better has been tossed around for a long time, and so far there is no answer. Personally, I prefer the natural fibers, but manufacturing processes in synthetics and blends have improved greatly, and many synthetic fabrics can be successfully used. Synthetics are especially good in the sheers, such as voile, organdy, chiffon, and batiste.

Choice of fabric can set the tone for your project. Calico, with its tiny sprigged patterns, has long been used in making quilts and is mainly responsible for what we call an "Early American" look. Bigger, bolder prints give dramatic emphasis to many appliqué designs. Geometric and floral prints both have a place in your stockpile; so, too, do the marvelous African cottons, the batiked, silk-screened, and tie-dyed fabrics widely available today.

Plastic and vinyl, fur, leather, suede, and their synthetic counterparts are all challenges for contemporary needleworkers; they broaden the scope and whet the interest. Whenever you see a piece of fabric or other material that appeals to you and excites your imagination, get some and hang on to it; you might not find a use for it for a while, but you'll have it when you need it.

FINDINGS

I'm using this word because I can't think of a better one. It refers to feathers, beads and buttons, braid, ribbons, laces, netting and veiling, seeds and seed pods, dried or artificial flowers and weeds. It also refers to tassels and fringe, sequins, bits of mirror or mica, bits of crochet or knitting, old costume jewelry, wire, shells, and all kinds of odd things that can be sewed to your appliqué, whether for whimsy or for realistic, three-dimensional effects. Don't get carried away, though, in experimenting; sometimes less is better than more, and such findings are meant to be merely accents, shadow rather than substance. Buttons and beads make dandy eyes for people or animals, or they can be used as flower centers. Fake jewels or sequins can punctuate a court gown in an appliqué

Andy's Patchwork Vest, by the author. Made of patches of Ultrasuede, real fur, fake fur, real suede, and leather, machine appliquéd to a medium-weight ground fabric. Vest is lined. Photo, Stubby Crowe.

Left: **This year, Daddy can wrap his baby in a bunting of luxurious ice blue Ultrasuede fabric. At the bottom, on either side of the front zipper, there are two little white Ultrasuede fabric lovebirds singing their hearts out to a pink rose. All machine appliquéd. The lining is blue polyester crepe, and the whole thing is washable and dryable by machine! Designed and made by the author. Ultrasuede fabric from Skinner. Photo, Stubby Crowe.**

Right: **Another Ultrasuede fabric gem, this time a luncheon cloth for the hostess with the mostess. In pale yellow, all machine appliquéd; in each corner a gray Ultrasuede fabric vase holds a bouquet of spring flowers in pastel shades. There are more blooms in the center. Designed and made by the author. Machine washable and dryable. Ultrasuede fabric from Skinner. Size, approximately 125 cm (45 in.) square. Photo, Stubby Crowe.**

portrait of royalty. Of course, you could use real jewels, too, if you had no other plans for the family treasures.

The biggest problem you'll have with these baubles, bangles, and beads is storage. Fabric storage is even more of a problem, and many a stout heart has paled in facing it. If you don't have a warehouse or a couple of extra rooms, start with a closet; add shelves if necessary and don't listen to the family's objections. Fabrics can be stored flat, rolled on tubes, wrapped on fabric boards, or slipped over hangers. Clear plastic shoe and sweater boxes work well for the findings we've been talking about; sort them before storing, and you can see at a glance what you have.

Your friends or family may not understand your determined collecting; you may get complaints. Try to make a deal, such as, "Don't touch my things and I won't touch yours."

SEWING TOOLS

Collect all your essential supplies and keep them in a box or basket where you can find them. Check what you already have and buy what you lack, for this will save time and temper later on.

1. **Needles.** For hand sewing, keep a varied selection—sharps in size 7 or 8, crewel needles from 3 to 9; egg-eye needles in size 9 or 10 for fine appliqué work; beading, tapestry (a blunt-ended needle), leather, and quilting needles. Quilting needles are short and sharp; a size 7 or 8 is a happy choice for hand quilting, but these needles work equally well for other types of sewing. I hope you have a sewing machine. If so, keep plenty of needles for it— sizes 11, 14, 16, and 18 for domestic models, and 70, 80, and 90 for imported ones.

2. **Threads.** I think all threads in recent years have declined in quality, but for hand sewing, cotton and mercerized threads are better than anything else. The introduction of polyester fiber in thread manufacture was a sad and frustrating event for hand sewers. The polyester threads tangle, knot, and fray; to offset this, run the thread over beeswax before you begin to sew. A little

round cake of beeswax in a clear plastic case with slots around the edges is available in notions departments. Get one, and use it all the time for both polyester and cotton threads; this light coating of wax will dry up those tears of frustration. Polyester threads work well on the sewing machine, however, so save them for this.

Aside from sewing threads, you'll need quilting thread, in colors as well as white. It is stronger than ordinary sewing thread and has been lightly coated with silicone for added strength and ease of sewing. Heavy-duty thread can be used for quilting, too. Add silk thread to your collection, size A or regular, as well as buttonhole twist, which is heavier.

3. **Yarns and floss.** Collect bits and pieces of all kinds and types of yarn and floss—nubby and smooth, thin and thick, rough or smooth. If you have a friend who knits—and who doesn't?—ask for some leftovers. Ask a friend who weaves to give you some thrums—leftover warping when a piece is finished. Your collection might include wool yarns, linen, cotton, mohair, acrylic, nylon, and orlon. Six-stranded cotton embroidery floss is almost indispensable. You can use from one strand to all six, depending on the effect you want. This floss comes in a huge range of colors and, happily, is available almost everywhere. It is also relatively inexpensive.

4. **Pins.** Use only good, sharp, rust-free pins. Stuff your pincushion full instead of keeping pins in the box; when they fall on the floor, you won't need to spend an hour picking them up. Keep pushpins on hand too; they are better than thumbtacks and you will need them from time to time.

5. **Scissors.** Few people realize how important scissors are in sewing and needlework; and even fewer possess scissors that are really sharp. You need at least three pairs. One pair of shears is for cutting fabric and a smaller pair is for trimming and cutting threads. If you have put off buying new scissors and if yours are dulled past recall, now is the time to splurge. *Splurge* isn't the right word; good scissors are an investment! Keep these for your work, and threaten the family if need be. You don't want any little darlings (or big darlings, for that matter) cutting up cardboard boxes or the garden hose with your sewing scissors. Your third pair of scissors should be kept for cutting paper or anything but fabric; never the twain shall meet.

6. **Thimble.** Not everyone is a convert to a thimble. I can't sew without one. If you don't use one, there will be many times when you wish you did—appliquéing heavy or stubborn fabrics, or quilting through three layers. They feel awkward at first, but persevere, for a thimble will keep your finger from getting sore, and you'll be able to sew faster and better in time. The thimble should fit comfortably on the middle finger of your sewing hand. You hold the needle near its tip, between your thumb and first finger, and push the end or eye of the needle through the fabric with the thimble. Some people use the side of a thimble, the way a tailor does; I use the end of it.

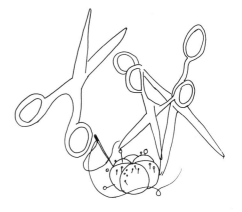

7. **Pens, pencils and other marking tools.** There are all kinds of pens and pencils, for writing notes to yourself and for drawing and marking. There are chalk pencils and heat transfer pencils. Add tracing paper, dressmaker's carbon paper, gum eraser, graph paper, tape measure, ruler, and T square. Dried soap chips work well for marking, too.

8. **Other tools.** Remember I mentioned how fickle memory is; get a notebook for your ideas, and use it. Keep a simple file for clippings, photos, ads, and drawings. Later you may want stretcher boards, frames, and hoops. Wait a while.

9. **Sewing machine.** If you don't own one now, you'll want one sooner or later—probably sooner. It doesn't take the place of hand sewing and hand appliqué; it adds to it, it is an extension. It gives different effects and it can be used alone, or with hand appliqué. A zigzag stitch is important; if you buy a new machine, be sure to get one equipped with it. If you have a machine now, but not a built-in zigzag stitch, you can purchase an attachment that will work well. Keep your machine in good working order. Read the instruction book and do what it says. Your machine is a good friend. Take care of it and it will pay you back.

10. **A place to work.** This is last on the list, but that doesn't mean it isn't important. Sometimes this can cause a problem. A separate workroom is ideal, but if you don't have that, start with a corner and a card table, and go on from there. This is an encroachment procedure, and if you are clever, your family won't realize you have taken over the playroom, den, or dining room until it's too late.

In any craft, there are many different ways to work. This is certainly true in needlework, and appliqué in particular, for the designs and fabrics are so varied. Methods and techniques change and combine as the need arises; what works well on one project won't necessarily be good for another one. This book was written for you. It covers a wide range of helpful suggestions and techniques, but the final choice is up to you. Don't be bound by one set of methods, for there really is no one right way to work. Whatever is easiest, most comfortable, and gives the results you want is right.

ENLARGING A DESIGN

Often you'll see a drawing or pattern too small for use in appliqué, and you'll need to enlarge it to comfortable size. These little patterns appear frequently in magazines, shown on graphs or grids. Using a graph in larger sizes is the easiest way to make the pattern bigger. For instance, if the drawing or pattern is shown on a 6-mm (¼-in.) grid and you want it doubled in size, buy or make graph paper with 13-mm (½-in.) squares marked off. If you want it four times the original size, use graph paper in 2.5-cm (1-in.) squares. If you have a problem finding graph paper in large grids, make your own with a ruler. Using shelf paper or brown wrapping paper, measure and mark the lines with pencil or pen. Art supply stores usually carry graph paper in assorted sizes; if there is one in your area, check it out first. When your enlarged grid is ready, refer to the original drawing or pattern and copy it, freehand, square by square. (See drawings, next page.)

If you want to use a design not pictured on a grid, such as an illustration or photo in a magazine or newspaper, then add your own grid. Mark the intervals on the design, and use a ruler to connect the marks. Using transparent graph paper will eliminate this step; art supply stores usually carry this. Place the transparent grid over the design you want to enlarge, then proceed to copy it on the larger grid as described earlier.

You can also use photo-enlarging to make a design bigger; this method is often used by craftsmen, especially professionals, but it is rather expensive. Margaret Cusack uses this for her fabric portraits.

4

YOU PAYS YOUR MONEY AND YOU TAKES YOUR CHOICE:

Ways to Work

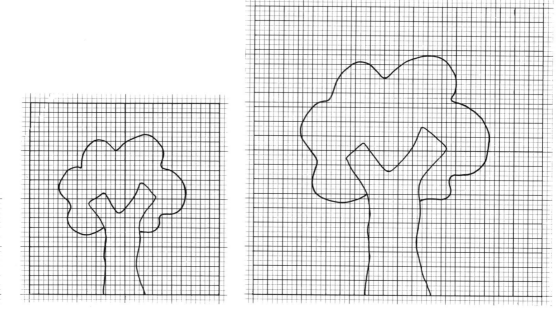

Enlarging a design with grids.

TRANSFERRING DESIGNS

There is no one, single way to work. Often, the project, design, or fabric involved will help you decide what method or technique to use, but if one doesn't work, you can always try another.

1. **Dressmaker's carbon method.** You can use this only on smooth, firmly woven fabric. Place the dressmaker's carbon paper, carbon side down, against the right, or face, side of fabric. Place your design or sketch on top of this, and be sure it is in the correct position. Secure these layers with weights or pins so that they won't slip or shift. Now, use a tracing wheel or stylus, or the point of a knitting needle, to go over the lines of the design. You will have to bear down with a little pressure to transfer these lines, but don't press too hard. Those little metal tracing wheels sometimes cut through the paper to the fabric and damage a thread or two, so try it out on a scrap first to be sure. When you have traced the design, remove the pattern and tracing paper. The transferred outline may be faint, but it should be sufficiently visible to follow easily, and faint lines are easier to cover. If there are some gaps in the outline, fill them in freehand with pencil or chalk.

2. **Tissue paper and thread basting.** This is a good method to use when your background fabric is heavy or nubby. Lay a clean piece of tissue paper over the design you want to transfer, and copy it carefully on the sheet. Now pin or baste the tissue to the right side of your fabric. Keep the work on a flat surface—a card table, your dining room table, or a kitchen counter. With contrasting thread, baste with small stitches through the tissue and fabric, following the lines of the design. A doubled thread may add a touch of security to this. Don't pull your stitches too tight. When you've finished, tear the tissue away carefully, bit by bit, so as not to disturb the basting stitches.

3. **The light method.** This method will not work with dark, heavy, or dense fabrics since they block out the light. You can use either natural or artificial light; for the first, a window or glass door

works fine; for the second, you can buy a light box, or make your own.

For either method, draw or trace your design on paper with a heavy marking pen. If you are using daylight, anchor the design to the window or door pane with masking tape, center your fabric over it, then secure the fabric with tape. The wrong side of the fabric will be against the right side of the design. Natural light shines through paper and fabric, and you transfer the lines to your fabric with pencil or chalk.

Ready-made light boxes come in several sizes and will plug in any outlet. They use fluorescent bulbs, which do not heat up, and they project the design the same way natural light does.

You can also rig up a pretty good light box of your own and save the purchase money. There are two ways to do this. First, get stretcher frames in the proper size and attach your ground fabric to them so that the fabric is taut and the tension is even. Put the right side of the paper design against the wrong, or back, side of the stretched fabric, and tape it in place. Use a small flexible lamp (gooseneck) behind it; the light will make the design outline clearly visible on the fabric and all you have to do is mark it. You may have to shift position once or twice to get each area of the design, but it is an easy way to transfer.

You can make a more permanent light box with a sturdy, heavy corrugated cardboard box and a single light bulb. Cut the top and bottom sections off so that you have an open-ended square or rectangle. On one side, along the bottom edge, cut a notch that will accommodate an electric cord. Prop the socket up so the bulb won't fall over and burn anything, then place the box framework over the bulb with the cord fitted into the slot at the side. You'll need a piece of glass to cover the open top of the box; it should be fairly heavy and large enough to extend a little beyond the sides of the box. Don't use ordinary window glass, for it could break with pressure. Get a heavier piece; although it would be more expensive, if you plan to use it several times it's worth the money—perhaps later you could use it in a tray or on an end table.

4. **Heat transfer method.** This also is for firm, smoothly woven fabrics. These transfer pencils usually come in pink or blue and are available in many notions departments or by mail at needlework supply houses. See that your original design is outlined in heavy black lines. If your design is balanced and symmetrical, with both sides alike, one tracing will be enough. If it is asymmetrical, you'll need two tracings unless you want a reverse, or mirror, image.

For the balanced design, place tracing (transparent, not carbon) paper over the marked design, and transfer the markings with the transfer pencil. Use a little pressure so that the lines are distinct. It might be necessary to go over some markings again; you don't want to lose them when you transfer them to fabric.

For an unbalanced design, or one you don't want reversed, you can do one of two things. Use the window method, but place the

"The Skaters" by Gladys Boalt. Detailed design was drawn first, then transferred to fabric with a light box. Background is brown and white geometric striped cotton; the oval shape is outlined with brown bias binding. Our lady skater wears a fur-collared blue coat, a long checked scarf, a bonnet, and a full, gathered tan dress. Her companion is resplendent in a double-breasted tan coat with brown lining, collar, and lapels. He also wears a gray top hat. Fine details are embroidered. The hanging is hand quilted. Photo, Stubby Crowe.

right side of the design *against* or next to the pane. If the lines are heavy enough, they will still be visible. Secure your tracing paper to the design on the window with masking tape, and trace the outline with the heat transfer pencil. This tracing will be reversed, so that when it is transferred to fabric it will come out facing the right direction.

If the window method is inconvenient, then lay the tracing paper over the design, on a flat, smooth surface. Use a regular pencil or pen for this tracing. Turn the tracing over so that it is face down. You'll be able to see the outlines clearly enough through the paper; this time, trace the design on the back side of the paper with the heat transfer pencil.

You're ready now to transfer the design to fabric. Be sure your fabric is pressed well and without wrinkles. Put it on the ironing board, right side up. Position the design properly, with tracing *down.* Use a fairly hot, *dry* iron—no steam—and use a lifting, up-and-down motion. The heat from the iron on the tracing paper will transfer the lines to fabric. Don't move the iron back and forth or the lines may smudge.

5. **Template method.** A template is simply a pattern piece. It may be whole or divided into parts. It can be made of metal, plastic, cardboard, sandpaper, or plain newspaper. It provides a pattern or design outline for you to follow. Put the template on your fabric and pin or hold it in place while you trace around it with regular or marking pencil. This is a very common and acceptable method in making quilts but can be used for most other projects, too.

Three appliquéd window tapestries by Fran Willner. This triptych was designed for dining-room windows, to be used during religious holidays. Fabrics in different weights and textures of natural tones, from interfacing to lace, appliquéd on beige linen. *Left:* **"Man and Woman in Their Environment."** *Center:* **"Man and Woman Alone."** *Right:* **"The Family." In designing these, Ms. Willner worked directly with cloth, rarely using a sketch or pattern. Most of the abstract shapes are created when the cutouts are removed, leaving negative leftovers. Photos, courtesy Fran Willner.**

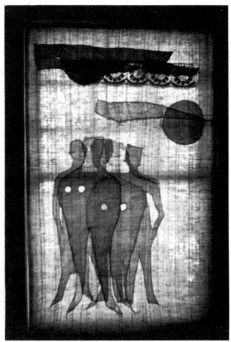

These five transfer methods leave outlines or marks on your fabric, which may or may not be a good thing. They make the design easy to follow, but you won't be able to change your mind at the last minute. You might—if the markings aren't too heavy or permanent. Pencil lines are difficult to remove; a gum eraser will help, but it may not take them away completely. Heat-transferred lines will wash out, but you certainly don't want to launder a newly finished piece. Also, your fabric may not take kindly to water. In method 5 we talked about tracing around a template. If you are skeptical about permanent or heavy pencil marks, try using soap chips. When you've worn a cake of soap down to a sliver, so thin it breaks in your hand, set the halves aside for a couple of days to dry. These are fine marking tools. They furnish a line definite enough to follow but easy to brush away when you're finished.

6. **Direct fabric method.** This means, in essence, that you work without benefit or restrictions of a prescribed design or pattern. It's a very exciting and spontaneous way to work, and it also increases your self-confidence. It's good to have a rough sketch first, showing placement of your ideas and indicating the size of your finished project. When you are working with wall hangings, banners, or fabric pictures, be sure to allow plenty of extra space around the sides. Cut your background fabric at least 5 cm (2 in.) to 10 cm (4 in.) larger than the finished size. Thread-baste your working or boundary lines inside this. This procedure isn't necessary for quilt blocks; this seaming or finishing is determined in advance, and 6 mm (¼ in.) to 10 mm (⅜ in.) is fairly standard.

Your background fabric should be pressed and free of wrinkles, and it should also be on the straight of grain. If it isn't, it won't lie flat. This applies to woven fabrics. The lengthwise grain runs parallel to the selvage edge of the material. The crosswise grain runs at right angles to this. Some cotton fabrics will tear easily along the grain, but test this on a scrap first. Most torn edges stretch or ruffle, and you'll be better off to cut. You can pull a crosswise thread to straighten the grain. Snip through the selvage, pick up a thread with the point of a pin, and pull. Occasionally you can pull the thread for the width of the fabric without its breaking, but most of the time a few inches is the best you can do. This pulled thread leaves a little ladderlike space; cut along this ladder to the end of it. Use the pin again to pick up the thread, and repeat the process across the fabric width. All of this is very important, especially for the background fabric; if the grain isn't straight, the piece will hang or lie crooked, and you don't want that.

It pays to experiment with bias in cutting appliqué shapes. When you place the lengthwise grain of the fabric at right angles to the crosswise grain, you end up with a triangle; the folded edge of this triangle is a bias fold and is very stretchy. Many times when

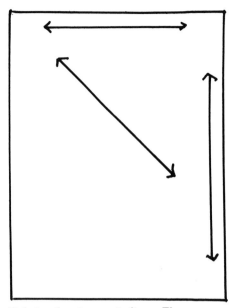

Fabric, showing grain lines. The horizontal arrow is the crosswise grain or warp; the vertical arrow is the lengthwise grain or woof; the diagonal arrow is the bias grain.

you are cutting out appliqué shapes, instead of laying the pattern piece on the straight grain, turn it so it is on the bias; when you take advantage of the bias grain, raw edges, and especially curved ones, are very easy to handle. Few people know how to handle bias properly, but if you take the time to practice with it, you'll be well rewarded.

If you want to work with an abstract design, instead of sketching first you might try cutting directly into fabric for your appliqué shapes. Cut the shapes larger than the size you have in mind; you can trim them later without sacrificing the design. This is a free-wheeling way to work, and it gets easier as you go along. Lay the ground fabric on a table, or tape it to the wall, and pin the shapes on. Move them around until you are happy with the placement; trim if they are too large. If one doesn't fit in, take it away. If a piece is too small and out of proportion, either cut another or add to the original. When you are finally satisfied with your design, it's time to pin, baste, and get ready to sew.

7. **The final transfer.** We've talked about several different ways a design can be transferred to fabric, and we've been talking about the background fabric. Most of the time you need the design in its entirety to act as a guide for you, but there are still the separate shapes to cut from the various fabrics you've chosen. You need two tracings of your design on paper; the first paper design will not only give you the overall picture, but you'll also use it as a transfer. Since the two paper patterns are identical, cut the second one apart carefully; use the cut pieces as paper patterns, and pin them to the selected appliqué fabric. Because the paper pattern is the finished size, you will have to cut outside this line to include a seam allowance or turn-under. From here on, it is an easy matter to match the appliqué shapes to the traced design on the ground fabric.

Fabric and design together will have the last word in deciding the method of working—not only in the transfer of design, but also in sewing, handling, and finishing.

Most small projects can be handled easily in your lap: pillows, tote bags, belts, pockets, book covers, eyeglass cases, and quilt blocks can be tucked in a bag or box, ready and waiting for you and some free time. These small things, happily, you *can* take with you—I try to leave one or two in the car all the time, just in case I should forget to pick one up while rushing out the door. We live in a mobile society, a rather frantic one; we meet trains, we take children to the doctor, the dentist, to swimming and ballet lessons; we go to meetings and are involved in countless activities. Waiting is inherent in these errands. Most waiting periods are frustrating and boring, but you can turn them into fruitful times if you have handwork. Fifteen minutes here, a half hour there, can accomplish wonders.

Larger projects, of course, are easier left at home. Whether you sew them by hand or machine or a combination of both, it is often

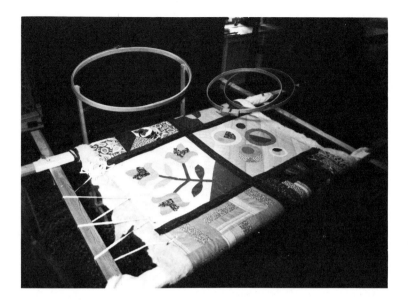

Small sampler quilt by the author, mounted in a homemade frame and fastened with C clamps. Also pictured are an oval quilting frame with floor standard and large embroidery hoops for use in appliqué work where even tension is needed. See Chapter 13 for additional details. Photo, Stubby Crowe.

too cumbersome to try to take them with you—and machine work has to be done at home anyway. My solution to all these little problems is to work on many projects at the same time; I'm not alone in this, for most craftsmen I know swim around in a pool of varied projects. This way you're never bored, and it's amazing how much you can accomplish.

FRAMES AND HOOPS

There are several different types of frames and hoops on the market—traditional frames for quilts, many smaller ones for smaller projects. I seldom use any of them, but I know many fabric artists who are uncomfortable working without them. Embroidery hoops come in many sizes, and some are sold in graduated sets. The hoops consist of two round or oval wooden or metal rings; the fabric, or whatever you are working on, fits over the smaller ring, which in turn fits snugly inside the larger one. An adjustable clamp on the outer rim holds it all in place.

Large hoops sometimes have a floor stand, and tambour hoops fasten to the edge of a table or counter. When you use either of these, both hands will be free to work. Quilters often use frames for quilting, although beautiful and very large quilts can be made without them.

You can improvise a working frame easily from an empty picture frame. Wrap the four sides with strips of muslin or heavy cotton, and baste the edges of your fabric or project to the cloth. If the frame is larger than the piece you're working on, pin safety pins at close intervals all the way around the fabric edges. Use cord or twill tape to lace the fabric to the frame—around the frame, through the safety pin, and around the frame again.

5

AS YE SEW, SO SHALL YE REAP:

Stitches of Appliqué

a. Running stitches. **b.** Blind or slip stitch. **c.** Whipping stitch.

HAND STITCHES

1. **The running stitch.** This is probably the easiest of all the stitches; it is also one that can be used on many different things and in many different ways. Running stitches of 13 mm (½ in.) or so are basting stitches—a temporary device to hold fabrics in place until you can sew them permanently. Small running stitches, 3 mm (⅛ in.) or even less, can be used to attach an appliqué shape to background fabric; it also can be used on hems or casings of hangings and banners. Keep in mind that it is visible. Because of this, it becomes part of the design and you should pay attention to the color and type of thread or floss you use in attaching the shapes. When you use a running stitch with a turned-under edge, be sure your stitches go through both layers of the fold; you don't want a raw edge to pop out when you've finished sewing. This stitch has several variations; an even stitch has the same length of thread on top of the fabric as underneath, or between stitches. An uneven stitch can have a tiny stitch on top, a longer one underneath (or greater distance between stitches), or you can reverse this.

2. **The blind stitch.** This is a traditional stitch for hand appliqué work, and when done correctly, it is almost invisible—in fact, that's how it got its name. Use a single thread, knotted, in a matching shade; come through the ground fabric from the wrong side so that the needle emerges slightly under the folded edge of the appliqué shape. The point of the needle goes *into* the fold of the turn-under, then back into the ground fabric right next to the place the needle emerged for the first stitch. Keep a distance of about 3 mm (⅛ in.) between stitches. This stitch gives appliqué a soft, rounded look and raises it very slightly.

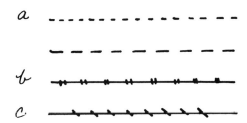

3. **The whipping stitch.** This is a very secure stitch, stronger than a blind stitch. For most fabrics, single thread is sufficient. Bring thread up, knotted, from wrong side of ground fabric, but *through* both layers of the turned-under edge. Insert needle back through the ground fabric at almost the same place, then bring needle up about 3 mm (⅛ in.) away for the second stitch, and repeat. The difference between this and the blind stitch is that the whipping stitch actually goes through three layers of fabric, and the blind stitch through two. Both stitches look similar from the wrong side of the ground fabric; both will be a line of slanted stitches. The whipping stitch is especially strong for sharp angles and points. This stitch shows much more than the blind stitch and gives a rather flat, crisp look to appliqué; it's important to keep stitches even and small or your appliqué may look messy when you've finished.

As mentioned earlier in discussing ways to work, there isn't any *right* way; also, there isn't any *right* stitch to use. It depends on what you're doing, the *effect* you want, the fabric you choose, and what is easiest for you. Some embroidery stitches can be used to sew appliqué in place, and we'll describe some of them later.

GETTING READY TO SEW

Pin the paper pattern pieces to the *right* side of the appliqué fabric and align grain lines. Trace around shape with pencil, soap chip, or dressmaker's pencil; then cut, allowing 6 mm (¼ in.) extra for turn-under or seam allowance.

Depending on fabric used, you can:

1. Turn under seam allowance and press in place before pinning to ground.
2. Turn under seam allowance and baste before pinning.
3. Pin in place and turn under seam allowance with tip of needle or seam ripper as you sew.
4. Stay-stitch appliqué outline first; this often helps with fabrics difficult to handle—especially synthetics and loosely woven fabrics. Use a machine stitch for this, about twelve stitches to the inch; use matching thread and stitch carefully around the traced line. It is easier to do this *before* cutting. After you cut, the seam allowance will turn under easily at the stay-stitched line; turn far enough so that the stay-stitching does not show.

SEWING CURVES

There are two kinds of curves—convex and concave. These are also called outside and inside curves. It is easier to sew curves on a lightweight fabric than on a heavy one. An inside, or concave, curve needs to be clipped before sewing so that it will lie flat. Use your small—and sharp—scissors for this; take tiny snips at right angles to the sewing line. The deeper the curve, the more snips you need. Stay-stitching helps here, and remember to do this before you cut.

Appliqué shape showing outside curves notched, inside curves clipped. Seam allowance is turned under along dotted line.

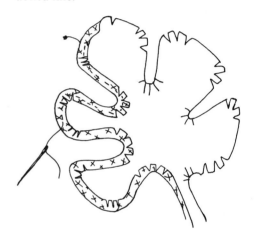

Wrong side of appliqué shape, showing notches and clips, and seam allowance partly turned and basted.

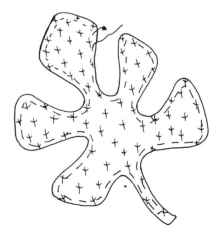

Right side of appliqué design ready for placement and sewing to background fabric.

It is easier to turn under the edges of a convex, or outside, curve, but be careful that you don't end up with a series of little points instead of a smooth curved line. Use your needle to work the fabric underneath as you sew.

SEWING POINTS

It's difficult to sew points and have them look neat; when possible, avoid them. If points are necessary to the design, here are a couple of suggestions. A right-angle point or corner is fairly easy to handle. Sew one side almost to the point, then tuck the other side under, and secure it with a stitch. This is called a two-fold turn.

Use a three-fold turn for an acute angle. As in the right-angled point, sew up one side almost to the tip end; this is first fold. Now, fold tip end horizontally across the point; this is second fold. Hold this in place while turning under left or other side; then secure all this with a stitch. Obviously, the smaller the seam allowance you have to turn under, the better the appliqué will look and the easier it will be to handle, so trim the seam allowance as much as possible.

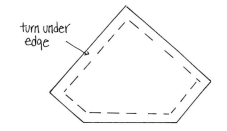

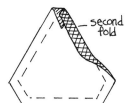

Sewing a right-angle point by two-fold method.

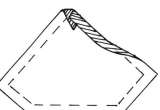
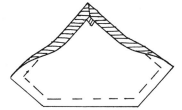
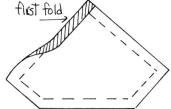
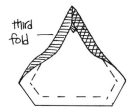

Sewing a right-angle point by three-fold method.

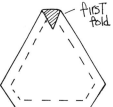

Sewing an acute-angle point by three-fold method.

SEWING CURVES AND POINTS WITHOUT FABRIC TURN-UNDER

These techniques, of course, do not apply to felt or other materials that need no turn-under. They also do not apply to some fabrics that, for one reason or another, are sewed with raw edges even though they fray or ravel. Heavy woven fabrics are too bulky to turn under; sheer fabrics show the turn-under, and this detracts from the overall appearance. There are two ways to handle sheers. First, before cutting out the appliqué, stay-stitch around the design line, then cut *very* close to the stay-stitch line. Pin appliqué in place on background, then sew with tiny whipping stitches or a running stitch just barely *inside* the line. The second method is to paint around the design outline with thinned-out white glue—just add a few drops of water to the glue, use a small watercolor brush, and apply the glue over the design outline before cutting. When the glue is dry, it will be transparent. Cut out on the line and attach appliqué. The glue keeps the threads in place and prevents fraying.

Nets and laces need no turn-under; they can be held in place with tiny tacking stitches. Both nets and laces can be used over appliqué, in whole or part, to tone down colors and give a muted, misty effect.

Some fabrics may lack body for a smooth effect in appliqué, especially with larger pieces. Slippery silks or nylons, gauzelike fabrics, or many synthetics fall in this category. Try a lightweight, nonwoven, press-on interfacing for this. Cut out the appliqué design of interfacing and do not allow for seam allowance. One side of the interfacing will be rough and perhaps look as if it were covered with pin dots. These little dots are resin, and the resin acts as an adhesive between the interfacing and fabric. Place the resin side against the wrong side of the fabric. Preheat a *dry* iron to medium setting, place iron on interfacing, and hold for a second or two. Do not move iron back and forth. Lift iron off, and let the fabric cool for a few moments, then cut around the interfacing, leaving a seam allowance or turn-under on the fabric, and your appliqué will be ready to attach.

This interfacing is made by several companies and is available at most fabric stores. It usually comes in black and white, so choose what is best suited for the fabric. Be careful not to get any resin on the sole plate of your iron, for it is difficult to remove. Try a scrap of interfacing on a sample first. If you think using it will change the character of the fabric, try appliquéing the shape to net or organdy with the raw fabric edge turned over the net; baste in place, then appliqué with your choice of stitches. This secondary background fabric is firm enough to hold a design—perhaps one consisting of several small, overlapping pieces—yet does not add unnecessary bulk. This method is often used for a beaded or embroidered design, or delicate appliqués. The design is completed on organdy or net; then it is sewed in place on the background fabric.

"My Country, 'Tis of Thee" by the author. Machine appliquéd in various cottons and felts on background of brushed denim. Felt scallops on edges of eagle's wings are detached, held by stitching on top side only. Photo, Virginia Avery.

Sewing circles. Cut circle larger than desired size. With a single thread sew running stitches around outer edge of circle; pull up on stitches, turning raw edge to inside. Circle can be stuffed lightly if desired. Sew folded edge of circle to ground fabric with blind stitches.

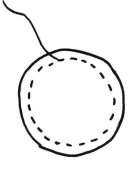

Chuppah (wedding canopy) by Fran Willner for Temple B'nai Abraham of Livingston, New Jersey. Two crowned lovebirds in purple brocade signify the bride and groom; they are quilted, jeweled, and embroidered with golden thread. The lovebirds sit on branches of the Tree of Life; the trunk of the tree is also quilted and is beaded with bird seeds preserved in polyester resin. Other flying creatures attending the lovebirds have gifts of flowers in their beaks. Sequined stars and a rhinestone moon adorn the top of the tapestry; fish and sea life, denoting the Creation, are appliquéd in velvets and brocades and covered by transparent turquoise fabric to indicate water. The Hebrew words "voice of joy, voice of gladness" are appliquéd in gold on the front panel of tie-dyed velvet. The Chuppah is approximately 7 meters square. Photo, Fran Willner.

Appliqué picture by Eleanor Loecher. Many different types of print fabrics are used here for texture and interest; note the overlapping and stuffed areas and the double borders of printed fabrics serving as a frame. Photo, Eleanor Loecher.

Some stubborn or so-called difficult appliqué fabrics will give interesting effects to your appliqué when you capitalize on their disadvantages. Play up frayed edges deliberately in certain designs; for instance, a yellow or orange burlap circle with frayed threads makes an effective sun in a daytime sky. Flower petals of frayed fabrics give a ragged but charming effect, and burlap, linen, or tweed can be used in this way.

ORDER OF SEWING

When you have appliqué shapes cut out and ready to attach, check the order of sewing. Certain parts of the design may overlap others. The edges of the underlying piece need not be turned under; they will be concealed, and turning the edges under would add bulk. Sew the underlying pieces first. For instance, the end of a leaf might be under a stem or flower; the body of a bird would be underneath part of the wing; a corner of a house or a fabric mountain might be underneath a tree. As you check your design, it will become obvious to you which sections should be underneath and which on top.

Some floral or weed stems and curved lines can be handled effectively with commercial bias binding. Since the binding *is* bias and will stretch, it is easy to use. It can be preshaped with an iron, or shaped as you sew. Sew the inside or inner curves first, then slightly stretch the outer curves into place and sew them down. Very thin stems can be handled with couched cords or yarns; this method will be described later.

MACHINE STITCHING: HINTS AND HELPS

Machine stitching is not necessarily faster than, nor a substitute for, hand stitching; it is different. It extends appliqué design and function into new areas. Projects you might never want to attempt by hand are possible on the machine, for it is easier to cope with heavier fabrics. Also, you seldom have to worry about turning the edges under, since in most cases the stitching covers the raw edges.

The two stitches used most for machine work are straight and zigzag. If your machine is old and does not have a zigzag stitch, you may be able to buy an attachment that will work very well. A zigzag stitch is as useful in many areas of home sewing as it is in appliqué and decorative work. A size 14 needle for a domestic machine and a size 80 for an imported one will handle most fabrics. If your material is very heavy, go to the next larger needle. Both mercerized and heavy-duty threads can be used on the machine, and it will also handle the polyester threads with ease. Whether you match or contrast your thread and fabric is up to you. Remember to start stitching with a full bobbin; it is maddening and frustrating to run out of thread in the middle of something, especially if you have to remove the work to rewind the bobbin.

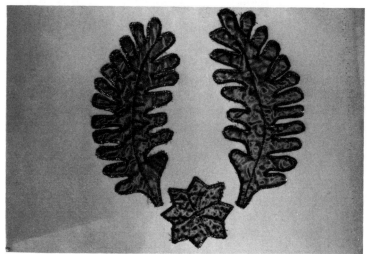

Above: "Winter Scene" by Jody Schnautz. Felt and cotton shapes are both hand and machine appliquéd to ground fabric. The effect of snow is achieved by using a layer of white voile over dark gray. The roof, of voile also, is lightly stuffed with polyfil. The figures of the children are felt; they are skating on a light blue pond. Borders are rust and blue with a print fabric between; the hanging is backed with Pellon fleece and a very little bit of quilting used for accent. The hanging is also lined. Size, 46 by 63.5 cm (18 by 25 in.). Photo, Stubby Crowe.

Above right: "Vase of Flowers" by Carole Pugliese. A corduroy vase machine appliquéd to a neutral background of smooth-textured linen. The lace flowers are made of antique doilies and set off dramatically by foliage and other blooms in bright to dark fabrics. The use of lace gives a light, delicate air to an otherwise formal picture. Photo, Carole Pugliese.

Right: These "Prince's Feathers" were taken from an old quilt design, but here they are shown as separate appliqués ready to sew on an evening jacket or skirt. Designed and made by the author. Red satin backed with silk organza for body; outline of feathers was traced on satin, then stitched by machine through both layers. Fabric was then trimmed very close to stitching line, and raw edges were covered with red overlapping sequins. Photo, Stubby Crowe.

Regard your machine as you would a dear and trusted friend. Accept its faults (if there are any) and get well acquainted with it. There is an instruction book for every type and model of machine. Read it, and learn how to operate as well as maintain your machine—clean it, oil it, and make simple repairs. If it *really* gets sick, call the sewing machine doctor.

You can use many of the same designs and fabrics for machine work as for handwork, although you may have to adjust the pressure gauge to accommodate different weights of fabrics. If the gauge is too tight, heavy materials will not feed evenly under the presser foot. For that matter neither will sheers. On older machines, the pressure gauge probably is a screw on the left top of the machine head; it can be loosened or tightened by turning. Newer machines have a pressure wheel, and often the wheel is sophisticated enough to adjust automatically to various fabric weights.

Both pin and thread basting can be used for machine appliqué. When using pins, place them at right angles to the stitching line so that the presser foot will glide over them, or, better still, pull them out as you come to them. Also clip and remove thread basting as the needle approaches; if you stitch over basting, the thread is difficult to remove later. Sometimes this happens in spite of precautions; if it does, use tweezers to remove the threads.

Large projects, wall hangings, draperies, or quilts are difficult to handle on the machine because of their size. Put a card table or chair behind the machine to support the weight. It is also difficult to handle the bulk of your work in the small area of the machine head. Roll the work up, if possible, and anchor it with safety pins so it won't pop undone when you least expect it. If you can stitch your project in sections, do so, and join the sections later.

There is overlapping and underlaying in machine work, just as there is in hand appliqué design. Treat it the same way. Sew the bottom, or underlay, first, but sew only to the points where the top layer overlaps; then stitch around the top shape. This stitching will secure both layers. If you plan to stuff or pad any of these shapes as you stitch, then remember to stitch only partway around, leaving a small opening; keep needle in the fabric, raise the presser foot, poke the stuffing through the opening, and complete the stitching.

Slow down for curves. If there is a reduction gear on your machine, use it. Lift the presser foot often to correct the position and direction of stitching. When you lift the foot, as described earlier, remember to leave the needle in the fabric while you pivot.

When you've finished stitching and removed the work from the machine, turn it over and pull the top thread through, then clip or tie. If you clip on the right side, some of the stitching may work loose, and you certainly don't want that after all you've been through!

A last bit of caution—before you start anything, test the stitching on a sample of the fabric. You'll be glad you did. This sampling may save you from folding your tent and creeping away into the darkness forever.

1. **Straight stitching.** Every sewing machine has a stitch gauge that regulates the length of the stitches. A 10 to 12 setting will do for most projects. Straight stitching appears as unbroken or solid lines in machine appliqué, and this linear effect moves the eye toward the dominant element in the design. A straight stitch, unlike the zigzag, will not cover up the raw edge of an appliqué

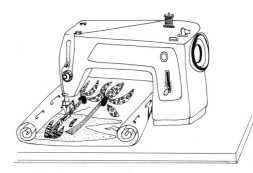

Handling a large project in a sewing machine. Top drawing shows design basted or pinned in place and project rolled from either end and pinned for security. Bottom drawing shows appliquéing by machine. This same technique can be used for machine quilting a finished appliqué.

Muslin café curtains with valance, by the author. Hand appliquéd in various cotton and cotton-blend fabrics. Photo, Stubby Crowe.

shape; this may or may not detract from the effect. In stitching a shape with raw edges, line up the cut edge with the far right side of the presser foot so that the entire foot rests on the appliqué fabric. If the raw edge is any closer to the needle or center position, the fabric will slip out of position, stitches will pile up, and you'll have wrinkles and pleats to fight. Leave yourself enough room, then trim excess fabric later.

If you want to turn the edges under, do it first and hand-baste it before you pin the shape to the background fabric. As you know, in hand appliqué, you can often turn the edges under as you go along; you can't manage this with a machine—not easily, anyway. So baste first, then pin in place, and stitch; this leaves both hands free to guide the work through the presser foot.

Pile fabrics are difficult to handle no matter what type of stitching you use; in machine work, try tissue paper underneath or between the layers, then tear it away later.

Many newer machines can stitch with two needles at the same time, and this gives interesting effects, particularly when two different colors of thread are used. The needles are set 3 mm (⅛ in.) apart; both use the same bobbin, and the bobbin stitch from the wrong side looks like a zigzag. You can use a straight stitch with various colored threads for random stitching across a design, but test your ideas first on scraps; you'll save time, fabric, and disposition, for machine stitching is difficult to remove once it is embedded in your fabric.

You can use the sewing machine straight stitch for free "drawing," too; a darning attachment makes this easy. You can drop the feed (the metal teeth that grip the fabric on the bed of the machine under the needle) on some machines and guide your fabric easily in any direction—read the instruction book for details, and experiment first.

2. **Zigzag stitching.** This is a marvelous stitch. You can regulate the setting from open and wide to close and narrow, and in between are all kinds of variations. As you shorten the length gauge, the stitches get closer together until they appear to be a heavy, solid line; this is a machine satin stitch and it will completely cover the raw edge of an appliqué shape, so that a turn-under is unnecessary.

As in machine straight stitching, be sure to position the fabric completely under the presser foot so that the entire zigzag stitch is on the appliqué shape. This is especially important in zigzag basting; use a narrow, open setting first. This secures the shape to the ground fabric and makes the project easy to handle. Then reset the machine for a closed zigzag or satin stitch, and cover the open basting and raw edge at the same time.

You can also attach appliqué shapes with two lines of open zigzag, using different-colored threads for each stitching. If your machine has built-in decorative stitches, or uses cams, try these out for varied effects in attaching appliqués.

A zigzag stitch, set wide and open, can also be used for couching. If you're not sure what couching is, you'll become acquainted with it in the section on embroidery stitches. At any rate, you can couch twine, crochet cottons, knitting worsteds, and some rug yarns with the machine, and this gives you a great textural dimension in outlining your work. Lay the couching thread along the basted line of the appliqué shape, following the line of the design; then set the zigzag wide enough to cover this. Most of the time you can guide the couching thread and machine without a problem, but if you need to secure it, use pins, and place them horizontally to the yarn or thread; otherwise, they could be lost to view and jam up your machine.

You're probably exhausted after reading this far—so much to learn about design, fabrics, and techniques of working. Don't get discouraged; remember to take one step at a time, and above all, keep your work simple. There's an old sailor's admonition (why it is attributed to a sailor I don't know) which we call "KISS"—and it means, in brash translation, "Keep it simple, stupid!"

As you experiment with appliqué, you'll find that just mastering a technique is not enough, and you won't get ultimate creative satisfaction or fulfillment by working another's design. You'll be emotionally and totally involved in all aspects of this as you get further into the possibilities, and this involvement, this attitude, will breathe life and vitality into what might otherwise be a sterile example of stitching.

6

CHAIN ME TO THY HEART:

Embroidery Stitches

Embroidery is almost as old as the proverbial hills, and the fascination and enthusiasm for this type of work is unabated. For centuries, embroidery stitches have been combined with appliqué, and needleworkers are constantly experimenting with new approaches and forms.

We can divide embroidery stitches into groups or families, and this is a nice, cozy way to think of them. The families, of course, are based on technique. There are hundreds of variations of the mother stitches ready to be plowed into the fields of embroidery, but we are not interested in all of these. In appliqué, we use embroidery stitches as emphasis, to depict details too small or too intricate to appliqué; we use them to embellish and enrich, and sometimes to cover, seams. When an appliqué has as much or more embroidery than it does appliqué, the piece falls on the side of embroidery or stitchery, so be careful of proportion. Know when to stop.

The "families" I mentioned are *flat, chained, looped,* and *knotted;* we'll use a few basic stitches from each group, but each will look different every time you change the texture, weight, or color of thread or yarn. The techniques are simple to master, but the direction is important.

FLAT STITCHES

The first is the **running stitch,** and by now you are familiar with it. This is the same stitch you used to attach some appliqué shapes, but it becomes ornamental when yarns and flosses are used instead of sewing thread. Sew from right to left in the stitch length of your choice. It will be a broken or dotted line; you can use it for outline or filling. Running stitches are really a series of straight stitches.

Right: **Running stitch, from right to left.**

Far right: **Running stitch as design outline.**

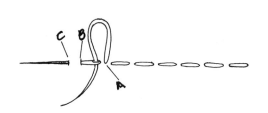
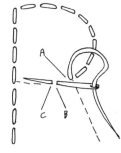

Straight stitches used in a circle can be flower petals, or, slanted, they become rain. A line of running stitches can be threaded, too; this means that an additional thread or yarn is woven in and out of the line of running stitches.

When straight stitches are laid next to each other to create a solid surface, this is known as **satin stitch.**

Outline or **stem stitch** is also in the flat family. The direction is from left to right, and the stitch gives a solid, instead of broken, line. While working this stitch, if the thread is above and to the right of the needle, it is *outline* stitch; when worked in opposite manner, with thread below and to the left of the needle, it is called *stem* stitch. It doesn't make any difference which you use, except that a convex curve is easier to do with the thread above, and a concave curve is easier to handle with a stem stitch, or thread below.

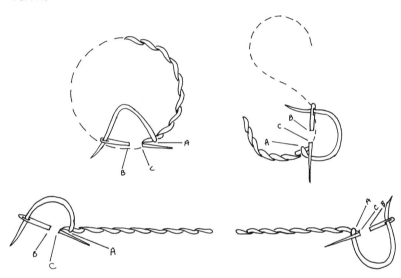

Far left: **Outline stitch (thread above needle) shown for left-handed people.**

Left: **Stem stitch (thread below needle) for right-handed people.**

The **herringbone stitch** is also worked from left to right. It's a very orderly stitch and most of the time marches along in geometric formation along two parallel lines, either straight or curved. Bring the needle up at *A* on the far left of the bottom line; slant the stitch to the right, take needle down at *B* on top line, then underneath and to the left and up at *C*. The thread crosses *AB,* and the needle goes down at *D* on the bottom line; repeat this to make a series of *X*-like stitches.

This same stitch is used frequently in sewing and dressmaking, but it is then called a "catch" stitch, since its purpose is to catch two layers of fabric together.

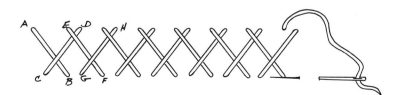

Herringbone stitch.

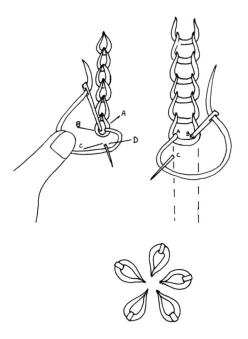

Top left: **Chain stitch, worked from top to bottom.**

Top right: **Open chain stitch, worked between imaginary parallel lines.**

Above: **Detached chain or lazy-daisy stitch.**

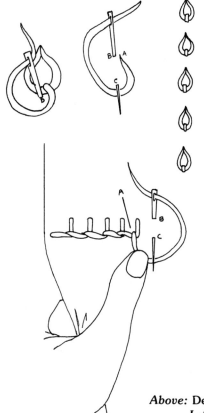

Above: **Detached chain stitch.**
Left: **Buttonhole stitch.**

CHAIN STITCHES

Chain stitch is very old, used the world over, and found in many museum examples from centuries ago. In the nineteenth century it was used extensively in Persian areas around the Caspian Sea; the chain stitch outlined a certain type of appliqué unique to the region—cut pieces of cloth applied to different-colored backgrounds but always outlined with chain stitch or couched cord. Peruvian children use this stitch exclusively in their colorful embroideries, as both an outline and a filling stitch.

This is a vertical stitch, and the direction is top to bottom. Your thumb plays an important part in working this stitch—the left thumb if you're right-handed, the right thumb if you're left-handed. Bring the needle out at A, and hold the thread below the needle with your thumb, forming a loop. Needle goes down at B, which is either the same as A or right next to it. Bring the needle out at C a stitch length away; C is inside the loop. Form a second loop and hold it with your thumb, then take needle down at D, which is either the same as C or right next to it, and continue in this manner. Keep the stitches loose so that the chain is easily visible.

A **detached chain stitch** is also called a **lazy-daisy stitch.** Start this the same way as a regular chain stitch; when the needle comes up at C *inside* the loop, make a tiny tacking stitch and take needle down at D, below the loop; CD holds the loop in place. An open chain stitch looks like a ladder. A regular chain stitch is worked on a vertical line, and an open chain is worked on parallel lines, either straight, twisted, or curved. It is worked in the same way, except that AB and CD are separated instead of close together.

LOOPED STITCHES

This family of stitches includes buttonhole or blanket, feather stitch, fly and Cretan stitches, and turkey work. Your thumb plays an important part in these stitches, too. If you don't hold the thread down until the loop is completed, the stitch collapses and you have to start over again.

Buttonhole and **blanket stitches** are really the same, except for spacing. Blanket stitches are farther apart. The direction is left to right, and this stitch also is worked between real or imaginary parallel lines. This stitch has wonderful variations; it can be worked as a border, in a circle, or to attach appliqué shapes. Bring the needle up at A, on the left side of the lower line, and hold the thread down with your thumb. The needle goes down at B, to the right of A but on the upper line. C is on the lower line, directly under B; needle comes out at C with the thread loop under the needle.

A **feather stitch** is worked like a buttonhole or blanket stitch, except that the direction is vertical instead of horizontal, and the stitches alternate from right to left along a single vertical line. Bring

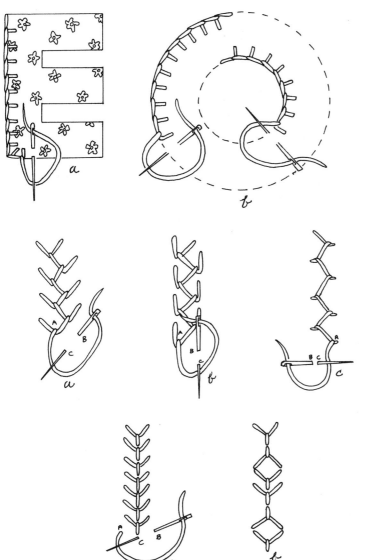

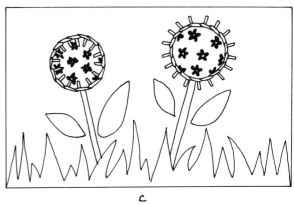

Above: **a.** Buttonhole stitch used to attach appliqué shape. **b.** Buttonhole stitch worked in a circle. Outer ring shows spokes pointing in, inner ring has the opposite. **c.** Variations of buttonhole stitches worked around flowers.
Left: **a.** Feather stitch, worked from top to bottom. **b.** Feather stitch, worked as a border between two imaginary parallel lines. **c.** Variation of feather stitch, giving an open, airy look.

Left: **a.** Fly stitch. **b.** Variation of fly stitch to show design possibilities.

the needle out at *A* at the top of the vertical line. *B* is to the right, and below; hold the thread loop with your thumb, insert the needle at *B*, and bring it out over the loop at *C,* which is below *A* on the same line. For the second stitch, throw thread to the left, go down below *A,* to the left of and below *C.* Continue in this manner. A double or triple feather stitch is made by completing two or three loops on each side before alternating. When the feather stitch is completed, the thread makes a wavy spine down the center line with stitches like little branches on each side.

   The **fly stitch** is often called a Y stitch—it looks like one. *A* is to the left of *B,* a little distance apart but on the same horizontal line. Make the loop as described for feather stitch, and hold it down with a tiny tacking stitch over the thread. You can vary this tacking stitch in length and give a different appearance to the stitch.

Top left: "God's Eye" felt hanging by the author. Letters in purple and turquoise with a few added shades on bottom of hanging; hand sewn with running stitches in black. The center of the eye is an oval beaded medallion ringed with rhinestones, appliquéd to an oval of pale blue felt, then in turn appliquéd to an oval of white; the blue-and-white layers are covered with gold mesh. The sparrow is in shades of brown, tan, and beige with white. The bottom border of beige is attached by French knots; triangles of purple were added for balance. Felt by G.A.F. Photo, Stubby Crowe.

Top right: Three-panel folding screen designed by the author. Felt panels are beige, 33 cm by 1.3 meters (13 by 64 in.). Center flower is red and pink, side flowers orange and gold, lavender and purple. Stems and leaves are bright green, couched with green herringbone stitches. French knots and straight stitches in black six-strand floss create flower centers. Felt by Continental. Photo, Stubby Crowe.

Bottom left: Felt "Peacock" hanging by the author, 56 by 99 cm (22 by 39 in.). Peacock in shades of orange, yellow, pink, red, and white, with a few touches of green. Embroidery in outline stitch and French knots. All hand appliqué. On black, with black felt border. Felt by Continental. Photo, Stubby Crowe. *Bottom right:* " Jonah," part one of a triptych by the author. Appliquéd on gray denim; trees are print fabrics covered with herringbone and open buttonhole stitches; ground foliage and waves (except for whitecaps, which are white felt) are various embroidery stitches, mostly couched yarns. Jonah's clothes are chain stitch, his beard detached buttonhole. Cretan stitches hold the nylon net cloud in place; the whale is black felt with embroidered eye and spout. Photo, Stubby Crowe.

Cretan stitch.

The **Cretan stitch** is fascinating and, used in any of its various forms, adds immeasurably to textural effect in appliqué work. As the name suggests, it came to us from the island of Crete, where it was used (and still is) to decorate skirts, vests, and blouses in bright colors. We know a good thing when we see it. The direction is vertical, and the stitch is worked like a feather stitch—but flatter, wider, and freer. You can change direction after you learn the stitch and work it horizontally, or around in a circle. In feather stitches, *BC* is slanted; in Cretan, *BC* is horizontal. Also, the stitches need not be underneath each other in a direct line; they can alternate from side to side for best effect. The stitch changes character completely as your direction and stitch length vary; it can also create a closed-in or widely spaced look.

Turkey work is also called a tufted stitch. Do not knot the thread, but leave the end free on the surface of the cloth above the first stitch, which should be small and worked from right to left. Take a second stitch to the right of the first, and return the needle to the starting point of the first stitch; do not pull the thread tight, but form a loop or tuft between each pair of stitches. These tufts, close together, make a dandy woolly fur for a little dog, yarn hair for a fabric person, or the center of a flower.

KNOTTED STITCHES

Only three stitches in this group concern us—the French knot, the coral knot, and the four-legged knot. Of these, the **French knot** is certainly the most important. It can be used singly or in clusters, with threads and yarns of any weight, and it can be very effective and decorative when used to attach appliqué shapes. Bring the needle up at *A*, then hold it horizontally and close to the ground fabric. Keep thread taut between thumb and forefinger of your left hand, and wind thread clockwise around the needle. Purists insist on one winding only, but often I wind the thread two or three times to make a bigger, flatter knot. Again, the choice is yours. Still holding thread taut with left hand, insert the needle at *B*, which is almost the same place as *A*—right next to it.

The **coral knot stitch** looks like a knotted outline stitch. It makes a lumpy line, and the knots that form the little lumps can be spaced regularly or grouped close together. This is a horizontal stitch, and you work from right to left, along a single line. Bring the needle up at *A*, then hold the working thread along the line to the left of *A*; use your left hand or thumb for this. Needle goes down at *B*, which is above the working line and a stitch length from *A*. Bring needle up at *C*, directly below line and the taut thread. With needle on top of thread, pull to form knot, then continue stitching.

Four-legged knot stitch is a single stitch. It looks like a plus sign (+) with a knot in the middle, and the arms of the sign are not always the same length. Using the plus sign as a guide, *AB* is the vertical line, with *A* on the bottom. *DC* is the horizontal line, with *D* to the left of *C*. Bring your needle up at *A*, go down at *B* and up at *C*. Now hold the thread horizontally from *C* to *D*; slide the needle diagonally under the two crossed threads in the middle, but do not take any fabric. With thread under the tip of the needle, pull the stitch tight to form a knot, then go down with needle at *D*.

Turkey work, or tufted stitch. Step 1.

Step 2.

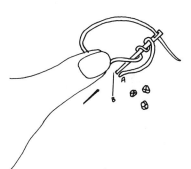

French knot.

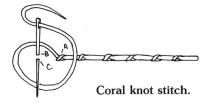

Coral knot stitch.

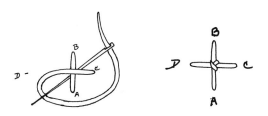

Left: **Making a four-legged knot stitch.** *Right:* **Finished coral knot stitch. Stitch from knot to *D* can be any length.**

Right: Jamaican appliqué, hand sewn. Charming native girl wears a large white hat, a bright blue blouse with white ruffles at neck and sleeves, a white apron over a dark red skirt. She carries a bouquet of embroidered posies in each hand, blue in the right, red in the left; her apron and skirt border are heavily embroidered, as are the flowers growing near her feet. Green and white fabrics represent ground; the design is appliquéd to soft rose denim. Photo, Mary Alice Fisher.

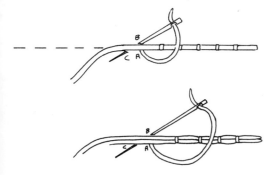

Top: Couching a single thread or yarn with straight stitches.
Bottom: Couching two threads or strands.

Couching two strands with cross-stitch.

Couching with open chain stitch.

COUCHING

The **couching stitch** is another of the old faithfuls. There are records of its being used as far back as the first century B.C. on Scythian embroideries. Since then it has been used in many cultures with many variations, for both outline and filling. Usually, in appliqué work, we use it for outlines. At one time, it was also called a "convent" stitch, perhaps for obvious reasons; we use the term *couching* now to cover almost all the variations. It is not really a stitch, but rather a means of attaching or holding down threads, yarns, cords, or other materials too thick or too uneven to pull through a ground fabric with a needle. You arrange one or more strands of yarn or thread along the outline you wish to follow and anchor it with pins at right angles to the yarn. Now choose a working thread to hold the couching in place. This thread is different from, and generally finer than, the couching thread; the holding stitches can be regular or irregular, straight or slanted. You can also couch with some embroidery stitches—buttonhole, herringbone, open chain, feather, and Cretan.

Couching is not confined to threads and yarns. You can couch rope, cordings, twigs, weeds, and dried grasses, but you must be sure your ground fabric is heavy enough to support them and the work will not sag under the weight.

Couching with buttonhole stitch. Couching with herringbone stitch.

During the early periods of on-lay work, almost all appliqué was outlined in couched thread, often of gold. The patterns were quite formal and contained. As appliqué grew in popularity and took on other forms, couching became a matter of choice; we use it now only when it contributes to design and effect.

STUFFED AND PADDED APPLIQUÉ

A little bit of stuffing under an appliquéd shape changes the whole appearance and often adds interest and a new dimension. The hair or face of a child or figure, the petals of a flower, the wing of a bird, or other similar objects lose their flat look and become soft and rounded. Polyester fiber-fil is fine for this, and it is easier to work with than cotton. Decide ahead of time which areas you want to stuff; sew around only three-quarters of the design shape, then poke the stuffing in carefully with a toothpick, a knitting needle, or the tip of a seam ripper. Work it into the outside areas first, then stuff the middle section; don't put too much stuffing in or your piece won't lie flat. When you've done this, finish sewing the appliqué shape to the ground fabric, thus closing the opening. It's a little easier to do this with hand stitches than with a machine, but if you are using a machine, hold the stuffing flat and away from the presser foot with your left hand while you finish the stitching, and you won't have any trouble.

Padded appliqué is similar in technique, but the effect is firmer and more sharply defined. Felt, Pellon, buckram, or even cardboard can be used for the padding. Cut this padding layer the *finished* size of the appliqué shape, then place the padding on the wrong side of the fabric that will cover it. As you cut the fabric, following the design, be sure to leave at least 1.3 cm (½ in.) all the way around for a turn-under. After threading your needle and knotting the thread, work from the wrong side and use a lacing stitch to secure the seam allowance smoothly all the way around. Alternate your stitches from one side to the other; when finished, your design will have a smooth edge, lie flat, and the padding will be locked inside the fabric. This is a good technique to use especially when working with a fairly large shape to give a smooth, professional look to the work. You can use a firm padding piece under a face, hands, tree, building, or anything that needs a sharp, flat outline. As you appliqué it to your project, work on a table or other flat surface. It is difficult to pin or otherwise hold a padded shape in place while you stitch it, and if you work in your lap, the shape may slip before it is anchored.

7

MORE WAYS TO SKIN A CAT:

Special Effects

Working flat will be easier, and you can hold the padded piece in place with one hand while you take the first few stitches with the other. If there are any embroidered details to stitch on the shape, be sure you do them before you put the padding in. Also remember that when you appliqué a padded shape, your sewing stitches go through the folded fabric edges, *not* through the padding layer.

DETACHED APPLIQUÉ

This is another little trick, and you can have some fun with it. Instead of sewing all the way around your appliqué shape, you attach it only in the center, or at one end or one side. Of course, this adds motion, motion adds shadows, and you get a completely new effect from this mixture. You can detach whole flowers, or single petals, leaves, animal ears, and tails, or other sections of your design, depending on whimsy and mood.

Some of you may remember Irene Castle from years back; she was the lovely wife and dancing partner of her husband, Vernon. She bobbed her hair and thus made the style acceptable to society in general. She also loved to wear and dance in loose, flowing chiffon dresses. One particular dress had a light and fluffy row of detached flowers around the neck, down the front, and around the hems of butterfly sleeves; this dress, of course, sparked a series of variations and copies, but even today, detached appliqué can change a plain dress or other garment into something special. You have a choice of method, depending on fabric and effect.

First, consider fabrics. Burlap, felt, lace and net, coarse tweeds and linens, leather, and suede and Ultrasuede need not be lined. A burlap garden or bouquet is wondrous to behold. Cut round or irregular shapes for both flowers and leaves, using appropriate colors; then fray and fringe the edges. Attach the flowers to the ground fabric in the center with a few French knots; if you stitch a tiny pleat in the center, the flower will stand away from the ground. Attach the leaves at the stem end, hiding your stitches by slipping the leaf end under the flower edge or stem. Instead of cutting out the flower in one piece, you can also cut separate petals; fray the edges as before, then attach them from the base end of the petal so that they overlap, and work from the center out. You can completely change the effect of this detached appliqué by changing the fabric. Instead of burlap, try linen, loosely woven wools, or tweeds. Also remember felt; the clean, smooth edges and velvety texture create a different look.

Areas of detached appliqué sometimes need to be faced, and this again depends on fabric and effect. You can cut a ready-made design from printed fabric, or use your own. Leave a wide seam allowance outside your design line; you can trim later. Place right sides of top and facing together, then stitch *all* the way around the outline by hand or machine. Now trim close to the stitching line,

Opposite: "Jacob" by Kopel Gurwin. ". . . The people bring him bread, and he drinks water from the stream. And after he goes to sit near the Jordan River." A striking, most imaginative and contemporary appliqué in felt, beautifully executed. Loops at top and bottom of hanging serve to hold it in place. Photo, courtesy America-Israel Cultural Foundation.

and make a little slit in the center of the facing fabric *only;* be careful not to cut through the top layer. The slit need be big enough only to turn the appliqué to the right side. A floral shape cut from printed fabric, or a flower cut from plain fabric, is equally effective, and a border around the neck and hem of a party dress

"Moon over the Mountain" by Judy Avery. The moon is tie-dyed muslin in orange and yellow, the sky is a blue print, and the mountain is dark green calico. Hand sewn and hand quilted. Photo, Judy Avery.

would be charming and different. When you have made the slit in the facing with your sharp little scissors, turn work carefully to right side, and work the seam to the outside edge with your fingers. Press if necessary. When you attach the center of the flower to the garment, the slit is underneath and does not show, and your design shape has a crisp, clean edge all the way around.

When lining or facing leaves—or animal ears, tails, or other similar shapes—stitch around them with right sides together, but leave the end open for turning. Turn, and either keep the shape flat or poke a little bit of stuffing inside to give it a rounded appearance. Then, as with unlined detached appliqué, sew the end of leaves slightly underneath the flower, the end of the tail underneath the animal or bird body, and tuck the raw edges of ears inside as you tack them in place.

QUILTING FOR ACCENT

Later on, there's a whole chapter on quilting, but right now I want to mention that quilting can add depth to whatever you are

"The Land of Green Ginger" by Maud Guilfoyle. Appliquéd of velvet, silk, satin, and cotton with delicate organdy nighttime clouds. Designed as a headboard hanging, it is accent quilted over polyester batting for depth. Photo, Maud Guilfoyle.

working on—wall hanging, banner, garment, or a small gift item. It's an extra accent and dimension. To achieve this, add a filler between the outside and the lining; this filler can be muslin, cotton flannel (preshrunk), an old blanket (if you're sure you won't need it for camping or the beach next summer), or it can be polyester batting, the kind used in bed quilts. If you quilt through two layers without a filler or middle layer, it's called "false quilting." When you quilt, you sew through all these layers—whether two, three, or four. You can use thread, floss, or yarn; it can match or contrast. If you quilt by hand, you can use a running stitch, or you can use embroidery stitches—any that strike your fancy and still serve to hold the layers together. If you quilt by machine, you can

"Genesis" by the author. Machine-appliquéd wall hanging in cottons, center areas padded and stuffed for a three-dimensional effect. Upper half of hanging represents day, bottom half represents night, with earth between. Photo, Stubby Crowe.

use a straight stitch with either a single or double needle, or you can use a zigzag or decorative stitch. We are concerned here with quilting as an accent, and this means that you don't have to quilt the whole thing, perhaps just one area of your design. Quilting will create a play of shadows on the surface as the light catches it, so decide ahead of time what you want to do before you plunge in.

The hanging "Genesis" (left) is a good example of some of the techniques you've just learned about. It is machine-appliquéd with closed zigzag or satin stitch, and much of the center area is stuffed. The sun's rays in the "day" section were done freely with double needle and two contrasting threads; the night sky at the bottom was quilted with a single-needle, machine straight stitch in a free-wheeling, crossed-line pattern.

SHADOW APPLIQUÉ

This is a delightful technique, one that gives an appealing, misty, and romantic effect. Use it primarily for sheer fabrics—voile, nylon, organza, chiffon, batiste, laces, and nets. You can use this for curtains, a freestanding screen, or room divider and have privacy without shutting out the light. It is equally charming used in an evening coat for summer wear, or a party gown for any season; you'll be the belle of the ball.

The method is easy; basically, the appliqué design is placed between two layers of sheer or transparent fabric and sewed in place. Although you can use any colors you like, white, off-white, or natural shades perhaps work better for this type of appliqué. You do, however, have a wide choice of both fabric and color for the design between the two sheer layers. You could try a white linen appliqué between two layers of white voile or organdy; you could also use laces, either cut to shape or, if you're lucky enough

Five sewing (or anything else) pockets by the author. Appliqués are all cut from various printed fabrics and attached by machine zigzag. Pockets are filled with polyester batting, lined, then machine quilted and bound with bias tape. They are designed to be worn around the waist. Photo, Stubby Crowe.

A felt appliqué hanging of a not-so-peaceable kingdom by Dawn Beecher. The wolf to the right looks ferocious enough, but he is held at bay by the scene before him—a placid, unsuspecting deer with her offspring. All felt shapes were appliquéd with embroidery stitches. Photo, Stubby Crowe.

"Partridge" wall plaque by Gladys Boalt. A mixture of fabrics in browns, both solids and prints, with accents of cream. The bird's wing is brown, machine appliquéd and hand quilted. The feathers are all detached appliqué, each one lined or faced back. The tail feathers are outlined with couched gold braid. Parts of the bird are stuffed lightly with polyfil; the completed bird was mounted on heavy cardboard. Photo, Stubby Crowe.

to have some doilies or medallions, used intact as your design element. You can also use felt or a printed linen or cotton in the middle, for the sheer fabric will cut the intensity of any color you have chosen. You can easily test the effect by laying the sheer fabric over the possible choices for the appliqué design, and decide whether or not you like the look. When you have made up your mind, cut the designs out, and lay them in place on top of the bottom layer of sheer fabric. Work on a flat surface. You need not turn any of the raw edges under in this appliqué, since it will be sandwiched between two sheers. Place the top layer on last, then baste or pin to hold everything in place.

Sew around all the lines of your design shape through the three layers, using a running stitch. Use matching thread if you don't want your stitches to stand out; otherwise, use a contrasting color, either sewing thread or a strand or two of six-strand embroidery

Right: A lovely example of true Broderie Perse, made by the late Florence Peto. Designs are carefully cut from eighteenth-century copperplate chintz fabric and appliquéd with tiny, almost invisible stitches to homespun fabric of the same period. The picture is finely quilted. Photo, Mary Alice Fisher (picture collection of the author).

Below: Modern-day Broderie Perse by the author. Bright bouquets from a printed cotton fabric were cut out and machine appliquéd to a deep blue sheet and pillowcases. Above the bed hangs the peacock banner, in the same colors as the appliqué below. Photo, Stubby Crowe.

floss. Remember to run either thread or floss through beeswax to make the sewing easier. Start with a tiny backstitch instead of a knot, and end with one too, or take your needle through to the bottom layer and secure the stitching there so that it won't show.

It is possible to eliminate a bottom hem on curtains by cutting your transparent material twice the finished length, plus 1.3 cm (½ in.) for turn-under. On each end of this rectangle, turn under a bare 6 mm (¼ in.) and baste in place, then mark the halfway line of the fabric with a basting across the width. Lay the rectangle on a table or other surface, and arrange your appliqué cutouts or design on the top half. Now fold the bottom half of the sheer fabric up over this so that the basting falls at the fold line. The basted ends should meet at the top; pin them together. Now pin the three layers in place so they won't shift, and sew them as described earlier. Use a running stitch to sew the top edges together, then make a second line of running stitches about 2.5 cm (1 in.) below this; you now have a casing for the rod. Barely turn under the side edges of the two layers, match them up, and sew either with slip stitch or running stitch.

BRODERIE PERSE

This technique involves cutting a design from printed material and sewing it to a background fabric. It dates back to the time America was still a young colony and fabric was scarce. Printed cottons and chintzes traveled from India to England and then to America; many people yearned for them, but few could afford them. The same was true of the palampores, the exotic printed cotton bed coverings made in India primarily for English use. A common pattern was the Tree of Life, but all the designs were lavish: elaborate flowers, trees, lush foliage, and marvelously plumaged birds. The colors were exquisite and soft, the dyes true. More often than not, women of early America could not afford either the palampores or the yardage, but they scrounged scraps and salvaged worn-out garments made of these prints. They cut out the designs carefully, no matter how small, and painstakingly sewed them to bleached—or unbleached—calico and homespun sheets; some sources attribute to this the birth of appliqué in America. This technique was called Broderie Perse, or Persian embroidery. No matter what it was called, it was an innovation, and from it sprang a whole new area of appliqué.

Today, we use the same technique for some of our appliqué,

Modern Broderie Perse, or print appliqué, by the author. Purchased napkins in rust-colored cotton-blend fabric are machine appliquéd with cutouts from a floral print fabric. Photo, Stubby Crowe.

Wall hanging by Eleanor Loecher. Machine appliquéd with a wide variety of printed fabrics in different weights, much of it padded and stuffed. Face "drawn" by free stitching on machine. Photo, Eleanor Loecher.

but we seldom call it Broderie Perse. Most of the time we designate it simply as printed appliqué. With an incredible range of printed fabrics at our disposal, we have unlimited selection for such work. All kinds of prints of definite design, traditional, stylized, or contemporary, can be used in this way—a figure, an animal, a bird, or a flower, anything at all. Cut out, they can be arranged to suit any whim, applied to almost any type of background fabric, and sewed down by either hand or machine.

RIBBON AND BRAID APPLIQUÉ

Fabric appliqué offers so many possibilities that it is easy to forget that appliqué can branch off into a little detour from the main road. Ribbons, braids, and tapes are all worth considering for appliqué; for the most part, the designs will end up in geometric shapes and angles, borders, and straight-line trimming; these, in their way, are just as effective as applied designs in abstract, traditional, or pictorial patterns. We've mentioned the staggering choice you have in fabrics, but it is no less mind-boggling to wander into the trimmings department of a shop and see rack after rack, row after row, and box upon box of these ribbons and braids. They are available in every color, both solid and patterned; they are also available in many widths, from 3 mm (¼ in.)

Left: **A skirt front before assembly, showing placement of ribbons ready for stitching. Ribbon or braid is sewed to the edge of the fabric, beyond the seam allowance to the unfinished hem.** *Right:* **The finished skirt.**

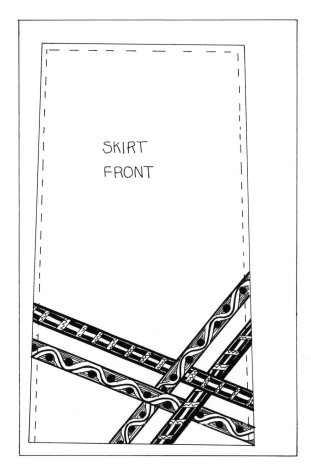

to 10 or 12 cm (4 to 5 in.), and can be had in silks, linen, wool, cotton, or blends. Ordinary bias tape used so universally in home sewing is one of the least expensive of these tapes, yet the color range is so extensive and so accessible that it offers unlimited possibilities.

Bands of ribbon and/or braid can trim blouses, shirts, skirts, slacks, and almost any item of wearing apparel. The same type of trim can be applied to many home accessories and decorative items—pillows, curtains, bath linens, sheets, and spreads. You can mix and match these trims to your heart's desire, and "odd" combinations often turn out to be the most striking. All of these trims have finished edges or, in the case of bias tapes, have pressed, turned-under edges, so only top-stitching is necessary.

FELT APPLIQUÉ

Felt is mentioned a number of times throughout this book, and rightly so; because no turn-under is needed, the sharpest points and angles and most intricate curved lines can be sewed with ease. It has one drawback, and that is minor: lighter-weight felts in particular tend to stretch. If you use felt as background for a large hanging or quilt, then back it with a piece of sturdy cotton or muslin; sew the two layers together around the edges and handle them as one.

You can get a sculptured effect by layering or stacking felt; sew a shape to a second piece of felt, then cut around the second piece, leaving perhaps a 1.3-cm (½-in.) border. Sew this to a third layer, catching only the second. Continue for as many layers as you want.

Felt can be adapted to almost any technique of appliqué. It can be sewed by hand or machine, covered with net or beads or embroidery; it can be stuffed and padded and fringed. It can be used for garments, for draperies, for upholstery, screens, pillows—the list is endless, and, above all, it's a pleasure to use.

"Jacob's Dream" by Kopel Gurwin. ". . . And he will lie in place and dream. And then there is a ladder on the ground of which the top reaches the sky. And God's Angels go up and down on this ladder." Large wall hanging of felt with stunning, lacelike cutout designs. Photo, courtesy America-Israel Cultural Foundation.

8

NOTHING NEW UNDER THE SUN:

"Pressed" Methods of Appliqué

In regular appliqué, as you well know, you sew fabric shapes to fabric background to form a design. You do the same thing in pressed work, but the difference lies in the fact that when you have finished, no background fabric is visible. Because of this, the choice of ground material is important only in that it supports the top layer. Most of this type of work is found in quilts and comforters, but much of it can also be adapted for use in small home items as well as clothing. The shape of the appliqué pieces determines the final design. Crazy patch, log cabin, spiderweb, and string designs all fall into this category.

CRAZY PATCH

This type of needlework came into vogue with the Victorian crazy quilts. These were very popular at the end of the nineteenth century. Made of velvets, silks, satins, and brocades, they were also richly embroidered over all the seams. These crazy quilts were not really quilts in the traditional sense; they were smaller than bed-size, and they were tied, tufted, or lined, rather than quilted. These quickly became status symbols; no well-furnished parlor was without its crazy patch throw, folded on the back of a loveseat or settee, or draped with studied abandon on a piano. The fad gradually disappeared, but crazy patchwork stayed on.

Its distinguishing characteristics are the irregularity of the shapes or patches and the variety of color and texture in the fabric. The pieces are fitted together willy-nilly, underlying and overlapping each other until the ground material is covered.

Here are a few tips to keep in mind. If you want to make a coverlet or large hanging of crazy patchwork, it is easier to do it in blocks or strips. Cut your background fabric, including seam allowances, and put it on a table. Now start in one corner and cover the corner with a fabric scrap and pin or baste in place. From here on, build out with varied scraps; remember to allow for a turn-under so that raw edges will be covered. Unless your fabric scraps are all straight-edged—which is unlikely—it will be easier to sew these down by hand. You can cover the seams or joins with a feather or herringbone stitch later if you want to, but it isn't necessary.

Almost any type of fabric is workable—silks and velvets mentioned earlier, cottons, wools, ribbons, and braids. Muslin or other inexpensive cotton or blend makes a good foundation. If you

Plate 1. "Windows on America," a 3-D appliqué wall quilt made by Betty Adams, Shirley Caulfield, Gladys Dickson, Fae Pierce, and Bobby Farrell.

Plate 2. A wall hanging for children, designed and made by Karen Lawrence. Machine appliquéd. Photo, Karen Lawrence.

Plate 3. Judy's "Taurus," by the author. Reverse appliqué, with embroidery. Photo, Judy Avery.

Plate 4. Two reverse appliqué designs by Martha Opdahl. *Left:* Flower Garden Quilt. *Right:* "Journey to Machu Picchu." Twelve layers of fabric cut through in two sections of six layers each. Photos, Martha Opdahl.

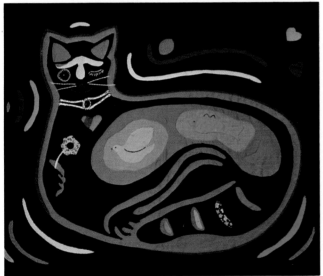

Top: Plate 5. A sharp contrast in appliqué techniques and effects. ''Playtime'' by Eleanor Loecher is machine appliquéd of various fabrics, many of them printed in overall designs. Photo, Eleanor Loecher. *Above: Plate 6.* ''Le Chat.'' Reverse appliqué by the author. Photo, Stubby Crowe. *Right: Plate 7.* Hudson's Christmas Quilt, an excellent example of fabric folk art in the business world. Designed by Nancy Kohlberg, hand appliquéd by Judith Wright. Photo, courtesy J. L. Hudson Co., Detroit.

Plate 8. Darien Bicentennial Quilt, designed and made by sixteen members of Goodwives Quilters. All designs were first appliquéd to organdy, then applied to background fabric. Hand sewn and hand quilted. Photo by Mary Alice Fisher, courtesy Darien Historical Society and Sue Heinritz.

Plate 9. Detail of Animal Quilt, designed and made by Susie Montgomery, hand appliquéd and embroidered. Mexican cotton used throughout with excellent placement and choice. Photo, Stubby Crowe.

Plate 10. "Tree of Life" appliqué quilt by Mary Belle Ostlund. Best in Show in Warren, Michigan, Quilt Exhibit, 1976. Photo, Mary Belle Ostlund.

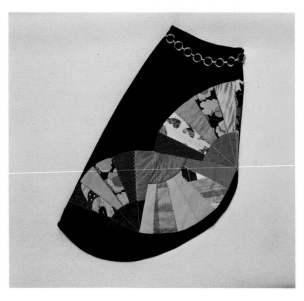

Plate 11. Fan evening skirt by the author. Scraps of wool, satin, and velvet appliquéd to black wool; embroidery added. Photo, Myron Miller.

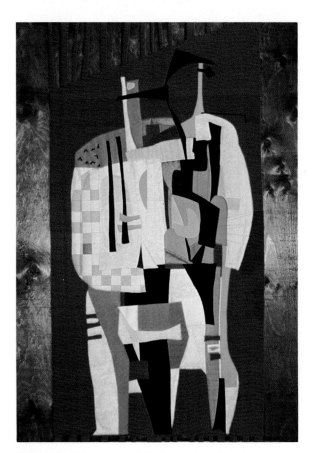

Plate 12. "Spirit of '76." Quilted wall hanging designed by Leslie Dor, made by Helen Squire for Dr. Eva Adler. Working from a small paste-up collage, Ms. Squire used a variety of fabrics from organza and chintz to wool, linen, and felt. Photo, Helen Squire.

Plate 13. Chair upholstered in crazy patch fabric made by Ardis James. The patches are all sample pieces of handwoven wool, set together on a sturdy foundation fabric. Photo, Stubby Crowe.

Plate 14. Westport Bicentennial Quilt, designed and copyrighted by Naiad Einsel, 1974, made by thirty-three women of the area. The center panel depicts the Minute Man statue in Westport. Hand appliquéd, hand quilted and embroidered. The quilt is owned by the Westport Historical Society. Photo, courtesy Naiad Einsel.

Plate 15. Putnam County Bicentennial Quilt, designed and coordinated by Gladys Boalt, made by eighteen women of the area. Both appliqué and quilting are exceptional, as are embroidered details. The quilt was made in sections and joined after quilting. Photo, Marc Cohen.

Steps in constructing a *crazy patch block.* The first piece of fabric is basted in place; the second piece overlaps it; the third overlaps the second; and so on. The completed crazy patch is shown at the end of the second row.

want to make an article of clothing of crazy patch, cut the pattern pieces first of muslin—the back, front, and sleeves. Arrange the crazy patches over each of these pieces, sew in place, then join the pattern sections together to make the finished garment.

The vest shown in Chapter 3 (page 25) is made of scraps of real and fake fur, real and synthetic suede. I found this easier to sew on the machine than by hand. You do not turn under the edges of such materials, but butt them together; a wide zigzag stitch catches both edges. Special needles for sewing leather are available for both hand and machine; they are wedge-shaped and will make the sewing a little easier. You'll need heavier thread, too. If you are joining leathers or furs by hand, you can simulate a zigzag stitch; alternate your stitches from one side to the other and pull the edges together snugly.

Below left: Detail of corner block in Victorian crazy quilt, begun in Boston, 1877, and finished in Haverhill, 1912. Shows embroidery stitches joining fabric patches. Courtesy, Tanya Taombs. Photo, Stubby Crowe.

Below: Crazy patch tennis racket covers by the author. Fabrics are a mixture of corduroy, cottons, and denim, also vinyl and fake fur, machine stitched on Pellon for body. Photo, Stubby Crowe.

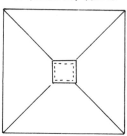

center square basted to foundation fabric

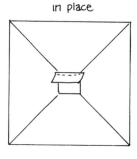

first strip sewn in place

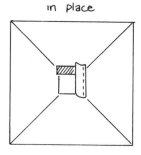

second strip sewn in place

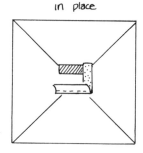

third strip sewn in place

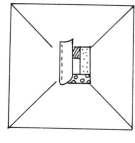

fourth strip sewn in place

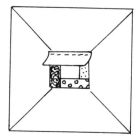

fifth strip sewn in place

sixth strip sewn in place

completed square showing light and dark pattern

Above: Steps in constructing a log cabin block.

Two arrangements for light and dark strips on log cabin blocks. *Left:* Strips placed opposite each other for "courthouse steps" setting. *Right:* Strips placed so that lights and darks are diagonal, for use in other settings.

Three settings showing arrangement of lights and darks on the diagonal placement plan. *Left:* "Sunshine and shadow." *Right:* "Straight furrow." *Below:* "Barn raising."

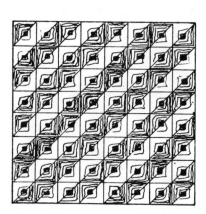

LOG CABIN

In sewing a log cabin pattern, you start in the middle of your foundation fabric instead of in one corner and build clockwise around a center square, called the "chimney" or "eye." This center square must be aligned exactly in true position on the ground fabric; otherwise the design will be crooked. Baste the eye in place, matching straight grain of the patch to straight grain of the ground fabric. All the rest of the fabric pieces are strips of equal width but staggered lengths. The first strip is placed right side down against one side of the center square and seamed through the three layers 6 mm (¼ in.) from the edge. This strip is then folded or pressed back over the seam, covering it, and the process is repeated around the entire block, alternating with light and dark fabrics. As the log cabin blocks are finished and joined together, they create a design, or "set." For instance, if the block is divided diagonally into light and dark fabrics, when joined they can become "barn-raising" or "straight furrow" or other patterns. If the darks and lights are separated horizontally, the design becomes "courthouse steps."

SPIDERWEB

Spiderweb and string patterns are both old-time quilt standbys, and their original design sprang from the urge to use up all the odds and ends of fabric scraps. The techniques are similar, but the approach is different.

For spiderweb, cut a block or square—say 30 cm (12 in.)—of lightweight cardboard to make your pattern. Subdivide it into four triangles by drawing two diagonal lines to opposite corners. Cut the triangles apart and mark one *ABC* as shown. Mark *D* as the halfway point between *A* and *C*. Measure 5 cm (2 in.) down from *B* on both sides, then join these marks with a line to *D*. This gives you a kite shape; cut it out for a pattern, and remember that it does not include seam allowance. Cut four foundation triangles of muslin, adding a 6-mm (¼-in.) seam allowance on all sides. Match the cardboard kite shape to the foundation triangles, and

A contemporary crazy quilt by Kathy Banker. Fabrics are velvet, satin, wool, and Ultrasuede joined to make an unusual circular design. Note embroidery covering the seams. Border strips radiate from center circle. Photo, Stubby Crowe.

Spiderweb block. Kite-shaped fabric placed on center point of four triangles cut from basic square. Seam strings one at a time on both sides of piece A until triangle is covered. Trim edges. Sew triangles together to make a square. Final design is a four-point star, with points midway on each side of the square.

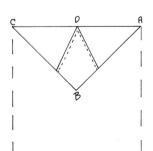 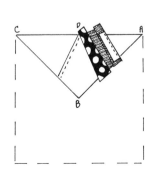 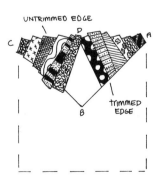 

trace around it with pencil. The finished design will be better if you use the same color for each kite. Use the penciled side of the foundation triangle as the wrong side. Now lay a piece of the fabric you want to use for the kite against the right side of the muslin triangle, and check to see that it extends past the pencil lines. Now stitch through the two layers, following pencil lines from point *D* to the marks on *AB* and *BC*. You do not need to stitch the uppermost corner at *B* since it will be joined in a seam later; trim any excess fabric away.

Spiderweb variations. Basic block is divided into squares instead of triangles; kite shape fits diagonally across working square. The four completed squares are joined so that points of stars are in outside corners.

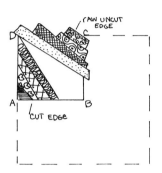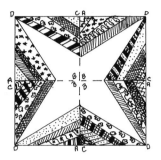

From now on, use the pressed method as described for the log cabin pattern. Work out from both long edges of the kite shape with strips of fabric until the entire triangle is covered; when all four triangles are, join them together to make a finished square.

You can vary the spiderweb pattern by cutting the 30-cm cardboard square into four equal squares instead of triangles. Mark one small square as in the diagram, then join the lines to make the kite-shape pattern. The difference in the finished version is just that the point of the kite meets the corner of one block and meets the middle of the side in the other.

STRING APPLIQUÉ

The string patterns again employ the same techniques for sewing strips in place, but the basic block is not divided into sections as in spiderweb. Leave it whole; it can be square or rectangular for easy sewing. This, too, is a scrap or salvage pattern, but it can be very dramatic and striking if color is planned ahead. It is also interesting to experiment with other geometric shapes as foundations—an octagon, a hexagon, or a diamond.

Start with a small fabric triangle in one corner of the foundation; pin or baste, then sew strips successively to cover the entire area. You work the same way with crazy patchwork, remember, except that the shapes in crazy patch are curved and irregular, while the shapes in string patterns are straight-edged. This is an easy one for machine stitching, too.

You can add interest to this design by inserting the same color at regular intervals, diagonally in the middle of your block, or perhaps at opposite corners. When completed blocks are joined together, the color repeat will form a pleasing repetitive design.

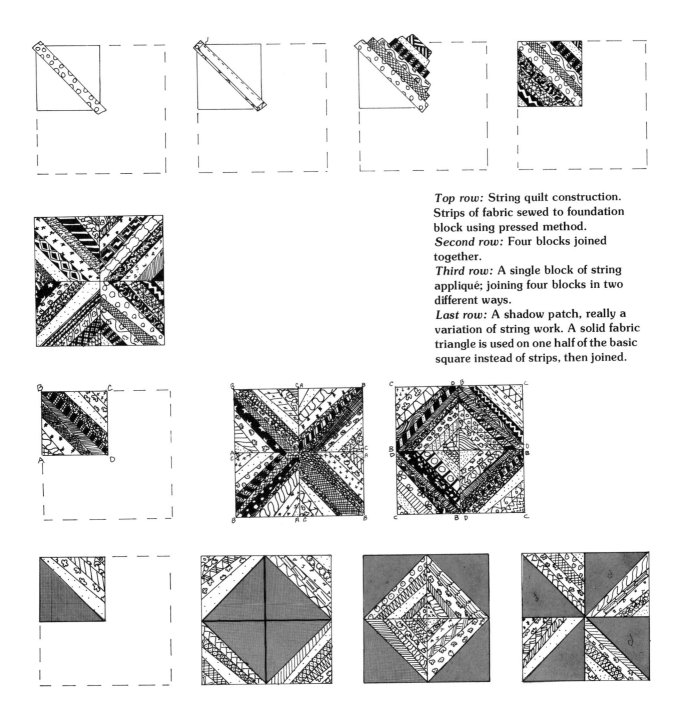

Top row: String quilt construction. Strips of fabric sewed to foundation block using pressed method.
Second row: Four blocks joined together.
Third row: A single block of string appliqué; joining four blocks in two different ways.
Last row: A shadow patch, really a variation of string work. A solid fabric triangle is used on one half of the basic square instead of strips, then joined.

9

NEW TRICKS FOR AN OLD DOG:

Reverse Appliqué

MOLAS

The term *reverse appliqué* is often confused with molas, those wonderful appliqués made by the Cuna Indian women of the San Blas Islands, off the coast of Panama. Mola work is not very old— it's a baby compared to regular and traditional on-lay appliqué, which goes back for centuries. As far as I know, mola work began about 125 years ago, and it evolved slowly from the tribal custom of body painting. As the outer world began to encroach on these Panamanian islands, starting with missionary visits, body painting gave way to painted cloth. Layered bands of cloth were sewed as borders on simple clothes or body coverings, ideas that possibly evolved from the Victorian period, according to some historians. These loose garments were gradually shortened to blouse length. Although the word *mola* actually means "clothes," we now use it to describe the particular type of appliqué these Indian women do. We speak now of a mola, usually a rectangle or square that can be used as wall decoration, a bag, or pillow front; we also speak of a mola jacket or skirt, referring to garments produced with the same techniques.

The ornamental borders first used by the Indians on the hems of their garments grew gradually to panel size; two panels, appliquéd with mirror images, were used for a blouse, one for the front, one for the back. The two molas were joined to a neck yoke and sleeves cut of different fabric, sometimes embroidered, and the sides of the molas were joined with a straight seam. There is a curious parallel between the customs of these Indian tribes and those of the colonial settlers of America. In those days a young girl was obliged to have a dozen quilt tops ready to quilt for her dowry. In the islands, a young Indian girl was supposed to have at least twelve new molas before she could present herself for marriage.

Another parallel lies in the source of designs; these overlap in all cultures and the final forms evolve as a result of the societies we live in. Nature, again, plays the most important role as the universal mother of design. Animals, birds, flowers, and trees are all used—they simply assume different styles and proportions. The Cunas also have deeply embedded religious beliefs, and these are evident in their work, as our religious symbols are evident in ours. They believe a spirit dwells within all natural objects; they draw on

Top and far left: **Although both of the mola panels appear to be complete, both will have a final layer of cotton added. Design already completed on underneath layers will be outline basted to top layer, then final layer will be cut and sewed in placed to reveal colors from underneath. Final detail of the lion will be a very fine chain stitch with one strand of embroidery thread, to complete face.**

Left: **A mola panel ready for top and final layer of cotton to be cut through and sewed in place. From the collection of Laurice Keyloun. Photo, Stubby Crowe.**

their imagination to picture this, and they portray their dreams and fantasies.

Captain Kit Kapp, in his book *Mola Art,* mentions that often the Cuna women, before they begin their appliqué designs, bathe their eyes and hands in a solution made from Sapi Karta leaves. This tree, with its long, elliptical leaves, grows in the mountains near the villages. These leaves are supposed to impart magic talent for artistic designs, and, judging from some of the work the women produce, it may well be so. Early molas were made with fairly heavy fabrics and coarse, uneven stitches, but gradually the mola makers refined their work; today it is unique. Undoubtedly, the tourist influx had an influence, for the women depend on this trade and consequently have raised the quality of their work.

The Cunas do not have a written language, but this has not hindered them. They are able to copy anything they see. Several years ago I saw a mola that was the exact duplicate of a Coca-Cola advertisement—it showed the appropriate bottle and glass with the command "Drink Coca-Cola!" An unhappy or whimsical invasion of the commercial world on hitherto unspoiled islands? I saw another mola recently that reminded me of that incident. A friend of mine returned from a visit to the islands and brought

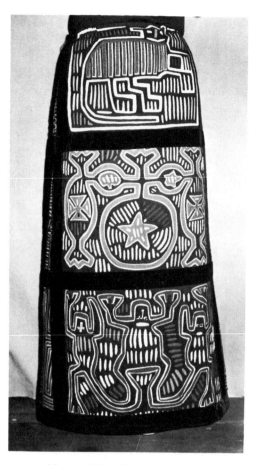

Above: Ellen Blanchard's mola skirt. Molas are joined together with strips of 5-cm (2-in.) black velvet ribbon; the skirt is lined. Designed by Beatriz Alacron, Bogota. Photo, Stubby Crowe.

Below: A mola panel, from collection of Laurice Keyloun. The design is the caduceus, the medical symbol. Photo, Stubby Crowe.

some molas back with her. One especially caught my eye; in bold, colorful, graphic lettering, it spelled out "Sex Relieves Tension."

True mola work is very fine; the slits of exposed color are even and incredibly narrow. When you examine one, the technique *appears* to be obvious. The colors of the design are revealed as *underneath* the top layer; consequently, you think of the colors as stacked, the design drawn; then, starting at the top, you would cut through one layer of fabric at a time to reveal successively the colors underneath. That is not the technique used by the Indian women; in fact, it would be impossible to turn out such finely detailed work using such a method. American women devised this technique, and it is clever and innovative; it has become known as reverse appliqué or cut-through work. Some stunning and exciting examples have emerged as a result, but it is not true mola work.

Indian women use from two to seven layers in their molas; more than seven layers are very difficult to sew because of the bulk. They use a cotton fabric similar to our broadcloth, in light- to medium- or dress-weight. The bottom layer can be and often is heavier, since it serves only as a foundation and is not cut. No matter how many layers the Indian women plan to use, they start with two. The two layers are basted together. The design is cut into the top layer, and the edges are rolled under and sewed in place, revealing the color of the foundation layer. Now a third layer of fabric, a different color, is added. A truly experienced needlewoman can *feel* the design with her fingers and cut into the third layer, following the lines of the already sewed design, roll under the raw edges, and sew the fabric in place, revealing the color of the second layer as well as the foundation layer. This process is repeated with each additional layer.

Extra colors can be easily introduced without adding the bulk of a whole layer; small pieces of fabric are placed on top of the layer just finished, then covered with the new uncut layer, which will be basted in place as described earlier. Slits are made in the top layer over the added pieces, then sewed down. This gives a mosaic appearance to the mola and creates a sculptured look.

This actual technique is little known in this country or outside the Indian territory, and it would be a novel and exciting technique for you to try. Start with four layers—that is plenty. Let's try it this way. The first layer (bottom or foundation) is orange; second layer, next to orange, will be white; third is red; and top and final layer is black. Start with an easy design, such as a fish or a flower. Keep the design simple. Draw it on paper cut same size as the fabric rectangles you plan to use, and color it to correspond with the four colors of your mola—orange, white, red, and black.

Begin with the white layer. Lay the red and black pieces aside until later. On the white, draw the sections of design that show the orange color. Lay the white fabric on top of the orange foundation block, and baste around the edges to keep the two layers together. Cut into the white layer only, roll the raw edge under

Mirror-image mola panel. Santa's face on left is of pink cotton; on right panel, purple cotton. Indian women often copy photographs and advertisements for their designs. Mola, collection of Laurice Keyloun. Photo, Stubby Crowe.

Left: Mola in production, showing final layer partially sewed down. Outline of animal is completed, and a few slits have been sewed to reveal color from underneath. Fabric shows cut slits ready to sew. Shaded pieces in lower left corner are patches of various colors basted together to make a second layer. The white outline of the animal is the bottom layer of the mola. Photo, Stubby Crowe.

Below left: Mola geometric design on a collar, showing three layers used. Choice of fabric here is unusual; it is satin, difficult to work with because of fraying. Photo, Stubby Crowe.

Below: Mola in progress. Final top layer of black cotton has been placed over the two underneath layers; design outline has been completed. Center portion is folded and pinned back to show design underneath; now, final layer both inside and outside design will be slit and sewed to correspond with design already completed.

with the tip of your needle, then sew the cuts in place with matching thread and tiny stitches. Now, on top of these two layers, baste the red (uncut) layer in place around the edges. Turn the stack over to the wrong side of the orange foundation; the stitches of the white layer should be clearly visible, outlining the design. Thread-baste in a contrasting color around the design, and then turn stack right side up. The basted line is your guide. Cut inside and/or outside, following your original design; sew the red fabric down, remove the bastings, then put the black layer on top and go through the process again.

If you don't trust yourself with the basting process, you can trace the sections of designs on each layer of fabric as you go, then follow the traced lines for cutting. In time and with practice, you will be able to handle intricate designs with this method.

TECHNIQUE OF REVERSE APPLIQUÉ

I'm not sure where the term *reverse appliqué* originated, but it is actually very descriptive. In regular or on-lay appliqué, we cut shapes from one or more pieces of fabric and sew them on top of a background fabric.

In reverse appliqué, we do the opposite. Shapes and colors are revealed by cutting down into successive layers of fabric; in using this technique for many years, here in America we've come up with some shortcuts of our own. Our designs aren't nearly as refined or as intricate as those of the Cuna Indians; nonetheless, they are good designs, and varied, and people are constantly experimenting for different effects.

For your first attempt, try a four-color stack of fabric as we suggested for mola work—orange on the bottom, then white, then red, and black on the top. Match up the sides and corners, then baste all four layers together to keep them from shifting.

Draw your design full scale on paper, and color it to correspond with the fabrics. You can transfer the entire design to the top since it will have to be cut away to reveal the under layers. One word of warning—if, for instance, you have traced the outline of a fish, don't cut around the whole design at once or the center will fall out; cut as you go, and pin where necessary, to keep the center parts of your design in place until you are ready for them.

You need sharp little scissors for this; you must be able to snip through the top layer without puncturing the one below. Keep your stitches as tiny as possible, and use matching thread, lightly waxed. When you have cut through and sewed down the black or top layer, revealing the red, it's time to cut through the red to reveal the white, and so on to the bottom. Stitch through all layers as you work.

I mentioned shortcuts before, but that may not be the right term; they are, at least, tricks of the trade! For instance, you don't have to reveal successive layers of color if you don't want to. You

Opposite:

Top left: Design idea from a bird design on an Ashanti urn; from *African Designs from Traditional Sources,* by Geoffrey Williams (New York, Dover). Four layers of fabric shown in shadings *A, B, C,* and *D.* First cutting from top layer, fabric *A.*

Top right: Fabric *B* is revealed. Designs in lower corners reveal fabric *C*—both *A* and *B* have been cut through here.

Bottom left: Fabric *B* has been cut through and sewed down to reveal fabric *C* in center shape and two upper corners.

Bottom right: Final cutting and sewing reveals fabric *D,* the bottom or foundation layer, which is not cut. Additional cuts and details can be made if you want them; also, additional colors could be introduced.

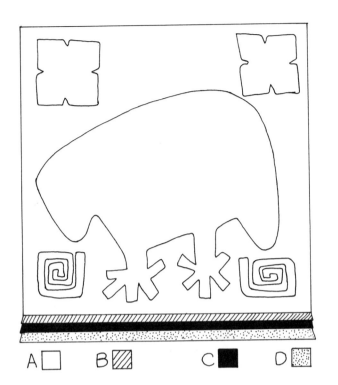

A ☐   B ▨   C ■   D ▦

A ☐   B ▨   C ■   D ▦

A ☐   B ▨   C ■   D ▦

A ☐   B ▨   C ■   D ▦

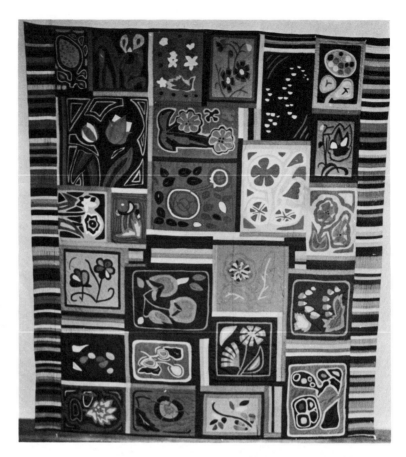

Flower Garden Quilt by Martha Opdahl. Reverse appliqué in bold, primary colors, patterns from Ruby McKim's flower drawings, here "exploded" and abstracted. This quilt won first prize in the *Indianapolis Star*— Wm. H. Black Co. quilt contest, 1976. Photo, courtesy Martha Opdahl.

Detail of the tulip design, upper left, from Flower Garden Quilt.

can skip a layer, or two, if you like. If you cut into the black top layer and want to show white instead of red, then make the same cuts into the red along with the black. It would be bulky to have to turn under the edges of both the black and red fabrics at the same time, so before you sew, trim the edges of red fabric *back* a little bit so they won't get in your way as you stitch down the black against the white.

Another trick is the introduction of other colors without adding a whole layer. I told you how the mola makers do this—they place the pieces of extra color on top of the finished layer, cover it with the uncut fabric, then proceed. When we want extra colors, our layers are already sewed together, so we insert the extras from the top; they must be cut slightly larger than the finished shape will be, but you poke them into the opening (carefully) and smooth out the piece until it is in the right position; anchor it with a pin, and sew the working layer down through the scrap and the rest of the stack.

Here's another trick. You have to be careful of your design— the lines cannot be too close to each other. For instance, when you cut a line into the fabric, if you turn under a 3-mm (⅛-in.) seam allowance on *each* side, the "line" will then be 6 mm (¼ in.) wide. Give yourself enough room. Study the drawings and the photos of the blocks Martha Opdahl made for her Flower Garden Quilt (see opposite and Plate 4), and you will see immediately that the design lines must be separated for this kind of work. Keep your lines at least 1.3 cm (½ in.) apart while you're learning. What you do later is your own business.

If your design has little circles in it, don't cut out around the circle; cut a little cross (+) into the fabric, then turn the edges under and sew them down—and the cross becomes a circle. If you are sewing a tiny square, cut an X into the fabric diagonally from corner to corner, tuck under the resulting triangles, and sew down.

Remember that the bottom layer of your reverse appliqué stack can be heavier than the others; it serves only as ground or foundation fabric and of course contributes to the color scheme, but you do not cut it. As to the fabric choice for this work, do try to find all cotton. The turn-under allowance is tiny, and a fabric containing polyesters will fray and cause problems. Aside from the fraying, it is difficult to turn under just a tiny bit of polyester-blend fabric; it keeps popping back out just as you think everything is under control.

So here you are, with a whole new pool to dive into; even if you aren't wearing a life jacket, you won't sink—you may end up having the best swim of your life. Martha Opdahl, whose work I mentioned earlier in this chapter, won the first prize in a quilt contest in 1977 with her Flower Garden Quilt all worked in reverse appliqué. This most certainly is a boost for this technique and I hope will encourage many others to try it, too. She is now experimenting with as many as twelve layers of fabric, holding many back while she works, cutting away unused portions to eliminate bulk, and also cutting so extensively into the top layer it is difficult to tell which color is dominant. "Le Chat" on page 20 is a good example of contemporary reverse appliqué. Try it; you'll like it.

10

LURE OF THE ISLANDS, MAGIC OF THE TROPIC SUN:

Hawaiian Appliqué and Quilting

The areas of appliqué are far-reaching, and boundaries are pushed back continually by artists and craftsmen experimenting with this medium. America is a country of quilt makers; quilting is an indigenous art, burgeoning now with a new explosive force. Quilt making is alive and well.

Hawaiian appliqué and quilt making are a step or so removed from the familiar forms of mainland America; island women have developed this beyond the craft stage into a unique art form. The Hawaiian quilt is one of the most intricate and sought after in the country; it is also one of the most difficult to do and do well, though it carries with it the pleasure of an unparalleled challenge.

The first missionaries from New England arrived off the coast of the Hawaiian Islands in 1820. While the missionaries were still on board ship, a welcoming committee of royal native women, the queen included, came to greet them. That must have been a most interesting scene. The missionary women wore high-necked, long-sleeved, tight-waisted, ankle-length dresses, as became the New England climate. Their female visitors wore wraparound skirts, made of tapa bark and decorated with designs, and from the waist up they wore only suntans. The least common denominator of this meeting surfaced almost at once. The missionaries wanted to cover up the half-naked Hawaiian women, and the natives were eager to have new clothes and set new styles. Languages were alien and communication difficult, except that needles and threads carry their own lines of communication.

One of the major problems in this early meeting was the queen's size—she weighed about three hundred pounds, and, indeed, most of her court were nearly as large. The missionaries, never ones to admit defeat, used a nightdress as a pattern and cut a full and flowing garment for the queen, using the full width of fabric they had brought with them.

This easy, comfortable garment became the muu-muu, which is still popular today. Once the great cover-up of the island ladies was accomplished, the missionaries turned to other activities— they began to teach quilt making to their new friends. They had brought with them a number of pieced quilts and bags of scraps, saved from the makings of their own clothes. The Hawaiians loved fine bedding and took great pride in the tapa mats they used for sleeping. The higher the social rank of the natives, the higher became the pile of mats. The New England quilts were novelties and curiosities, and the island women were eager to learn how to make them. Records of early quilt making tell us that for a number of years after the missionaries arrived, quilting bees were held regularly. Also, according to the accounts, quilting frames were used, high ones for the New England ladies who liked to sit on chairs, and low ones for the native women who preferred to sit on the ground.

As far as any of us know, these early quilts were pieced, and almost from the beginning there was a built-in problem. Quilt making in America began as a salvage craft, a necessity, and the

79 · HAWAIIAN APPLIQUÉ AND QUILTING

Hawaiian quilt, deep green on white. A traditional, intricate design. Notice the fine "wave" quilting throughout. Photo, Camera Hawaii, courtesy Mauna Kea Beach Hotel.

"Lu'u Hae Aloha" ("My Beloved Hawaii Flag"). Hawaiian flag quilt with royal coat of arms appliquéd in center medallion. The flag quilts usually portray a flag on each of the four sides; there are eight stripes, one for each of the Hawaiian Islands, patterned after the American flag. The crosses of Great Britain are shown in the canton; this stems from the period after the War of 1812, when the Hawaiian flag was originated. Many years later, the flags were incorporated in quilts, since the Hawaiians feared that with the fall of royalty they would no longer be able to fly their beloved flag. Photo, courtesy Honolulu Academy of Arts. Quilt is a gift from Mrs. Richard A. Cooke.

Opposite: Deborah Kakalia demonstrates traditional Hawaiian quilting, seated in front of one of her finished quilts. Courtesy Ala Moana Americana Hotel, Honolulu. Photo, Graphic Pictures Hawaii, Inc.

missionaries carried with them the same message of thrift. They had not reckoned with the size of the Hawaiian women, however; it took a full width of fabric to make a dress or muu-muu, and there literally were no scraps left. The native women began to think it slightly ridiculous to cut a length of fabric into little pieces, then sew them all together again. No one is quite certain when the idea of the Hawaiian quilt actually came into being; like many ideas whose "time has come," it probably gradually evolved. Some accounts attribute it to the time of the birth of the royal prince, in 1858. There is, however, a charming little folk tale connected to the origin of Hawaiian appliqué design.

The tale concerns a native woman who spread a large muslin sheet on the grass to bleach in the sun. When she went out in late afternoon to get it, she noticed the sun was casting shadows across the sheet, shadows of the leaves of a nearby bush. The design of the shadows was so captivating, so lovely, that the woman immediately cut out the pattern, and thus Hawaiian design, as we know it now, was born.

There could well be a great deal of truth in the tale. Hawaiian women are by nature happy and carefree, living in easy accord with the lush growth of nature around them. Their designs come from this—trees, flowers, and shrubs are all incorporated into their quilt making; they do not use animals or birds in their work, and their approach to appliqué is unique.

In familiar areas of appliqué, we cut designs from different

pieces of fabric, then combine them to form our pattern on background materials. We work with comparatively small sections sewed together to make a whole. Not so the Hawaiians. Their designs are large, sometimes covering the whole center of the quilt. They use solid colors, selecting two of high contrast. Many early quilts were made of the turkey red cottons appliquéd on white; later, red and gold, the royal colors, were commonly used. They do not use black.

Designs originated in Hawaii are treasured and passed from mother to daughter; the name of the design is passed along, too. Although nature is the greatest source of their designs, they draw on symbols and signs as the rest of us do. When the queen abdicated, and the Hawaiians felt they might not be able to fly their flag again, they incorporated the flag design into a quilt. These quilts have a great uniformity of design—four flags used in each quilt, one on each side. Often in the center is the Hawaiian coat of arms. These are the only quilts using more than two colors. They have also used the queen's comb and the queen's fan as sources for stylized designs. From design to technique, these quilt makers have devised their own unique form, and now many of us are learning from them, adapting their methods to our needs and uses.

The Hawaiians use solid colors; most quilt makers in the rest of the country use a combination of solids and prints. The Hawaiians seldom use the block method of assembly, preferring to cut and sew one large, bed-size pattern. Appliqué is their medium, their

Hawaiian appliqué wall hanging by the author, appliquéd and ready for quilting. This is a traditional design by Deborah Kakalia, here done in rose pink on cranberry. Lower right corner shows layers of batting and backing. Photo, Stubby Crowe.

nature best suited to the freedom and flowing lines of such design. Many experienced quilt makers cut directly into their fabric, but whether they use paper patterns or not, the technique—best described as a snowflake technique—is the same. As children, we learned to fold paper and cut delicate and intricate patterns; as grownups, we still use this method, finding new directions and new uses for such lacy and elegant designs.

Start small; those words by now are familiar to you. A 46-cm (18-in.) square is a good beginning size. From your stockpile of fabrics, choose two colors of sharp contrast—red with white or

83 · HAWAIIAN APPLIQUÉ AND QUILTING

Two more Hawaiian designs. From the collection of the Mauna Kea Beach Hotel. Photo, Camera Hawaii.

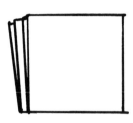

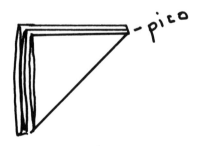

Folding paper to cut a pattern, Hawaiian style. First fold is horizontal; paper is folded again to make a square; folded edges are then brought together to make a triangle.

gold, pale blue on dark green, or orange on brown; you pick it out. You'll need a square of each color, cut to the same size. One important thing to think about here, however, is fiber content; use all cotton for the appliqué. You can use a poly-cotton blend for the background or base, but *don't* use it for the appliqué; the difficulty in sewing it will take all the fun out of your work.

Cut a square of paper the same size as the fabric—46 cm (18 in.). Fold the paper in half horizontally, then fold it again to make a smaller square. It will now be one-fourth the original size. Crease the folds carefully so that they will be exact. You will have cut edges on two sides of the folded square, and folded edges on the other two sides. Bring the *folded edges* together to make a triangle—the long side of the triangle is the bias; the short side is the straight. The point of the fold is the *pico*, or the center of the design. The design is cut between the two *folded* edges of the triangle, toward the center, in a continuous line. There are many Hawaiian patterns available today, but it's a lot more fun and a lot more interesting to cut your own. When you finally have one you like, it's time to transfer it to fabric.

Fold your all-cotton square the same way you folded the paper, and finger-crease each fold carefully. You might also use a pin or two to keep the fabric in place; if it slips, you ruin your design and have to start over again. When you've completed all the fabric folds and now have a triangle that corresponds to your folded paper pattern, pin the paper securely in place; you're ready to cut. This may be difficult, for you are cutting now through eight thicknesses of fabric, and it is absolutely essential to have sharp scissors. If you still have problems cutting, unfold your paper pattern and your fabric triangle and use the square. Pin the paper even with the folded sides of the fabric square; the main arm, or ray, of the design will line up along the bias, with the shorter elements on the straight. Now cut, and when finished, remove the paper pattern. Unfold your cotton design and place it right side up on a flat surface.

Next, prepare the base or background square. Press it, then finger-crease it diagonally in both directions. If you are using a blended fabric for this, it may not take a finger crease. Fold it diagonally and thread-baste along the fold in a contrasting color so that you have a large X from corner to corner of your square. You need this guide to align your appliqué. The diagonal or bias part of your design will line up with the arms of the X on the background; center it, smooth it carefully into place, pin it, then thread-baste. Often in sewing appliqué, pin basting is enough, but don't try it with a Hawaiian design—the pattern is too big, and you save time and patience in the long run if you baste. Baste crisscross first, then around the outline about 13 mm (½ in.) from the edge. Don't turn under the raw edges ahead of time. Roll or tuck these under as you sew—use the tip of your needle or the back of a seam ripper. Sew angles and points as you come to them—don't fold under ahead of time. Also, though you'll be working with curved lines, it seldom is necessary to clip these curves; the bias cut of the fabric has enough "give" that the work will lie flat after sewing. Also, the turned-under edge of Hawaiian appliqué is less than other types—at the most, 3 mm (⅛ in.)—so you do not need to cut extra for a seam allowance.

When you've sewed down your appliqué, press the square and get ready to quilt it. By now, I think everyone knows what the quilting process is—you sew separate layers together with a quilting stitch. In quilt making you have a top (which is usually pieced or appliquéd, sometimes embroidered, painted, or batiked), a middle layer, and a bottom or backing. The middle layer is some kind of filling—wool, or an acrylic blanket, cotton flannel, or cotton or polyester batting. Since the advent of polyester batting, most other fillers have lost popularity, for this filling is easy and even to work with, is washable, and, all in all, is a definite boon to quilt makers everywhere.

These layers—top, middle, and bottom—are basted together, then sewed with fine, even little stitches through the three layers until the entire area is covered. The quilting stitches, whether running stitches or stab stitches, are the same as those used by other quilt makers for fine quilting; the difference is in the design. Traditional American quilting patterns were based on grids and usually are variations of some form of geometric shapes. Hawaiian quilting is contour quilting; it follows the outline of the appliqué design in parallel lines about 13 mm (½ in.) apart. This contour quilting covers not only the appliqué shape but the background as well; some say the flowing lines remind the native women of the waves of their beloved Pacific Ocean; indeed, the quilting is often called "wave" or "echo" quilting, "luma-lau" in Hawaiian. We borrow this technique from the Hawaiian quilt makers and use it in many other ways; often, outline or contour

Below left: Folded paper (or fabric) with design (shaded) drawn ready to cut. *A* is the pico, or center point of design; *AB* is bias or diagonal fold; *BC* is outside edge; *CA* is folded edge on straight grain.

Below: Design appliquéd to background square. Dotted lines show two variations of contour or echo quilting which could be used in the design area. Contour quilting on background would fill up rest of block or square.

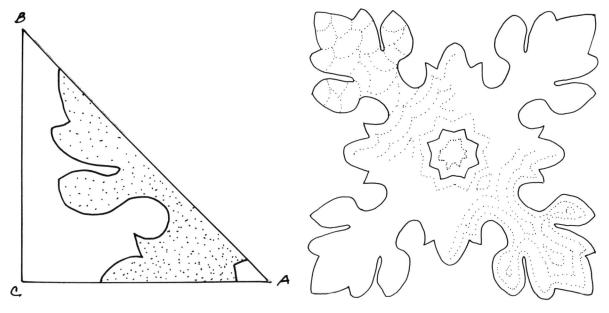

quilting adds necessary stature to many varied types of appliqué designs.

Hawaiian quilts have long been such a striking force in the needlework field that it is hard to imagine Hawaiian appliqué without the quilting that makes it so distinctive; yet, as we explore and experiment with so many different techniques and approaches, we're finding more ways to use the appliqué technique alone. We've already discussed making a square or block of a single design; such finished squares make lovely pillows; they can be used as tote bags, table mats, or card table covers, and the designs, modified, are stunning and effective on clothing. Fabrics other than quilt maker's cotton can be used, too. Felt is a wonderful medium for such appliqué use; apply it to a long evening skirt of flannel or tweed, or use it on a poncho or cape. A Hawaiian-type design, in whole or in part, can be used for and on almost anything where other appliqué is suitable.

After trying Hawaiian appliqué, you may like it well enough to want to make a quilt but, understandably enough, may hesitate because of the size—such a large design, such bulk to handle and later quilt. It's nice to know that, once more, there are no set rules. Plan your quilt using the block method if it is easier for you; you can duplicate the appliqué on each block, or you can make each of them different. Working piecemeal has its advantages; when you have enough blocks for a quilt, join them together and go on from there. Work in the most comfortable way for you.

Quilts could well be the most popular area of appliqué today. Quilt making itself is a force to be reckoned with—no longer a closet craft, it is out in the open and marching along near the head of the needlework parade. Quilts are part of the American heritage, and they speak with loud and clear voices of the women who made them. The appliquéd quilts of the mid- to late nineteenth century raised the standards of quilt making to hitherto unknown heights; with the abundance of good fabrics and the discovery of the curved line, imagination and talent soared in this medium of personal expression. There was a freedom here not found in the repetitive disciplines of pieced geometric work.

A tremendous variety of quilts emerged from that period, and, in a way, they have influenced greatly the quilts made from that time to the present. Many were made of what we now call traditional patterns: stylized formal designs, usually floral, in wreaths or geometric arrangements planned to fit on a block. Some appliqué quilts we can classify as presentation quilts—quilts made for a bride, made for a neighbor moving away, made for a minister by his congregation, made for a friend as a token of love and esteem. The album quilts were the friendship quilts, almost always signed with embroidered names. The bridal quilts were usually the most elaborate, with intricate and elegant designs and incredibly tiny stitches. A young man reaching his twenty-first birthday often received a freedom quilt, symbol of his years of work bound to his father and recognition of his arrival on the threshold of responsible adulthood. It seems to me that in this day and age, someone should start a trend of making freedom quilts for women.

The appliqué quilts with perhaps the most appeal and greatest impact were the pictorial quilts; these often showed unlimited imagination and a personal perspective that at once commanded respect—looking at some of these old, prized quilts is like looking through an open door to view a person's private life.

Few can be classified or tucked neatly into a category outside the word *pictorial.* Most have a strong emotional appeal; some have the flat and linear quality we think of as folk art—a lack of perspective that has its own appeal. Harriet Powers, a former slave, in the late nineteenth century made two such quilts depicting Bible stories, unusual events, and scenes from her own lifetime. Both quilts are unique, both show a straightforward

11

COME ONE, COME ALL:

The New Quilts—Any Number Can Play

The Johnny Appleseed Quilt, made by the "Settlers," a group of women quilters in Ft. Wayne, Indiana. Quilt depicts the life of John Chapman, born in 1774. Chapman was a legendary folk art figure; he carried a knapsack and Bible, wore a cooking pot on his head, and traveled over the countryside giving away apple seeds and seedlings. Photo, courtesy Rachel Misegades.

approach to life and its problems, and both have forever immortalized the simple, honest woman who made them. One hangs now in the Smithsonian Institution, the other in the Museum of Fine Arts in Boston. Another outstanding example of the pictorial quilt is the famous Civil War quilt now in the collection of the Shelburne Museum in Vermont. It was made by a hospitalized soldier recovering from battle wounds. Here again is history recorded, a creative thread unbroken.

Folk art has many definitions; about the only thing unchallenged about it is its universal appeal. It has great originality, no matter what the medium; those artists, folk or otherwise, working then or now in fabric have an unsophisticated and natural approach to their work. They do it to please themselves, and the rest of us benefit; we see an innocence, a naïveté, a primitive but delightful effect.

Quilt making, like many other crafts, was pushed aside for many years; but it never died out, and countless quilt makers throughout the country remained completely unaware and uninterested in the fact that it was no longer a popular pastime. It slumbered on until just a few years ago—around 1969 and 1970—and then was awakened with renewed vigor. New York

City's Whitney Museum presented a show called "Abstract Art and the Pieced Quilt" that shocked artists, craftsmen, collectors, dealers, and everyday people into a new awareness of quilts and of their priceless quality. It was a New York woman, however, a talented craftswoman and ardent conservationist, who is largely responsible for giving the appliqué quilt a good swift kick—a kick that sent it reeling from darkened wings into the footlights.

The woman's name is Irene Preston Miller, and she owns a charming and successful craft supply shop in New York, the Niddy Noddy, located near the Hudson River. For years Irene Miller agonized over the river's decline, seeing its majesty dissolve in pollution and neglect. She wanted to dramatize its need and get the public aroused so that they would take corrective action; her solution was a pictorial quilt, the now-famous Hudson River Quilt. She wanted it to portray different aspects and scenes of life on or around the Hudson River. She provided bright blue broadcloth for the fabric river and green broadcloth for trees and landscape; these two colors served to unify the quilt's design.

Mrs. Miller then invited other women to join her in the project; they planned the scenes or pictures for the blocks, with each woman responsible for appliquéing and quilting a square in the thirty-block quilt. Plenty of publicity, promotion, and news stories followed every stage of the quilt's progress, for it represented a novel approach to a social cause.

It took three years from idea to finished quilt, but in 1971 the quilt made its debut and was an instant success. It was written about, photographed, and exhibited all over the country as well as in Europe. It not only pointed up the need to clean up and restore the Hudson River to its former majesty, but it opened new horizons for quilt makers. They saw in it a fresh new concept, the quilt moved from the bed to the wall, no longer strictly functional but now a decorative focal point. It was the occasion of America's two hundredth birthday, however, that propelled quilt making, meteorlike, across the country.

America planned a long time for its birthday party. Most of these plans involved art and sculpture, historical exhibits, dramas, concerts, and community events. Money was also available for restorations and refurbishings of public buildings and places. Comprehensive as the plans were, they still did not, and could not, include all the towns and villages scattered throughout the country. Everyone wanted to get into the act; enter—the Bicentennial quilt.

Here was the perfect answer. Communities, associations, clubs, and library and historical groups could now participate actively in the celebration and, what's more, contribute to posterity. The Hudson River Quilt was their model. Here were group involvement, community sharing, community creativity, and community pride all wrapped up in quilt making. Here, also, was something to be proud of long after the concerts and exhibits had faded from memory. These quilts would hang in the courthouse, or the library, or the town hall, or the local museum—in fact, they do now; the Bicentennial quilt answered a great need for people to be heard, to be counted, and we have so many, they roll in waves over America from sea to shining sea: stirring portraiture, early and current scenes, industry and nostalgia, all sewed together to make a picture of America.

Almost all these quilts are appliquéd. The usual format was a scene based on history. Sometimes a professional designed the entire quilt; more often, interested quilt makers, men and women alike, met to discuss and plan the contents and continuity, the patterns and overall design, and each person was often responsible for researching and designing a block. If someone couldn't draw well, help was available from others more talented. The quilt makers shared fabric, sewing skills, and confidences. They learned to work together, to handle grievances and the inevitable problems that arise from group participation, and they ended up with lasting mementos of a newsworthy period.

There is an unfortunate aspect in these quilts; you see so many of them that sometimes they all look alike—and many of them are. There is an inevitable similarity. The Bicentennial quilt mak-

Town of Deerpark Bicentennial Quilt, designed by Mrs. Isolde Arcier and made by twenty-seven women of the area. First-prize winner, 1976, at Orange County Fair. Photo, courtesy Shirley Zeller and Town of Deerpark.

Drawings of three block designs for the Westport Bicentennial Quilt, now owned by the Westport Historical Society. Drawings, enlarged to correct size, were cut apart and used as patterns. See Plate 14 for photo of quilt. Designs by Naiad Einsel, a professional artist.

ers ran head-on into this problem, and there was no sidestepping it because there is not enough variance in the typical early scenes or events of young America. They built the same homes, farms, and factories, they fought the same battles either with nature, man, or selves and made their own history with only minor differences. Many of the quilts are exquisitely worked and planned, but what really distinguishes them is the set—the final, overall design. One hundred years from now, many of these quilts will be on exhibit again; the viewers will shake their heads in astonishment, but they'll know more about their country, their local areas, their politics, and their fellow man than ever before.

Of course, the Bicentennial quilt wasn't the only type to emerge

"Save Long Island Sound" Bicentennial Quilt. Each circular motif represents one town or village on Long Island, with highlights and name of community appliquéd and embroidered. Circles were then appliquéd to blue denim background and hand quilted, with a Mariner's Compass design between the circles.

from this renaissance. From earliest America, quilt making has been a dominant form of self-expression; it is no less so now. Old patterns, methods, and techniques were hauled out and dusted off—and looked at with critical eyes. As a result, quilts hang on corporate walls, advertise and promote products and services, and, as always, express personal opinions and social climates.

One marvelous contemporary example of this is the "Watergate Quilt," made by Mildred Guthrie of North Carolina. There have always been good periods and bad periods in history, and there always will be, but never before in human records have so many catastrophic changes occurred *so fast* as in present times; we can hardly catch our breath from such shattering blows. Think of the past seventy-five years or less. We've had three disastrous wars, one Great Depression and a few smaller ones; we've lived through one of the ugliest and most shameful political scandals in our history. Our faith in country, leadership, and established order has been violently shaken. Our ideals have been shattered, our moral precepts undermined, discounted, and laughed at; our private lives and sexual attitudes have been probed, examined,

criticized, and publicized until we are all drained. Americans, though, are a resilient people. The old song says, "Pick yourself up, dust yourself off, and start all over again." We may be enraged and disillusioned but we prevail, and something of this sentiment is expressed in Mildred Guthrie's Watergate Quilt. I quote from her account:

"In the center of the quilt is a portrait of President Nixon. A piece of net has been placed over his portrait representing the veil of secrecy which surrounds his alleged knowledge of the cover-up. If and when the Senate votes not to impeach the President, the net will immediately be snipped away. Encircling the portrait is a rotating circle of accusing fingers pointing in every direction. The fingers do not point to anyone in particular. Not until all evidence has been heard and the courts decide must the finger fall on the guilty person.

"Black clouds have been added because Attorney General Saxbe stated, 'Historians will record Watergate as a black cloud in American History.'

"There is a border of fifty stars representing the fifty states.

Above left: "George Washington at Valley Forge," by Chris Wolf Edmonds. Idea from a *Saturday Evening Post* cover of 1975, painted by J. C. Leyendecker. Center medallion uses both regular and reverse appliqué; the entire quilt is hand sewn and hand quilted. It won first awards in several shows, and when it was entered in the Kansas State Fair it won first in the Bicentennial quilt class, the Sweepstakes award for quilts, and the Stearns and Foster Mountain Mist Best-of-Show award. Photo, courtesy Chris Edmonds.

Above: Detail of the "Freedom Rider" quilt, a pictorial appliquéd quilt commemorating Paul Revere's ride. All hand sewn, by Chris Edmonds. Photo, courtesy Chris Edmonds.

Onondaga County (New York) Bicentennial Quilt, all hand appliquéd and hand quilted, by twenty-five women. Octagonal blocks depict growth and development of the county, and the squares represent plants and wildlife. Photo, courtesy Mary Helen Foster.

These are shining stars. Watergate has been disastrous for us, but we must not let it tarnish America. Interwoven around the stars is the Watergate tape. There is an 18½-inch gap in the tape representing the 18½-minute gap in the original tape.

"Now! It is no secret what is in the gap. Ye little quilt maker has used this space to stitch her name. Senator Baker and Senator Ervin share equal space on the pillow. Featured on the drop are Watergate scenes framed in the tape.

"Because of the wrongdoing of Watergate, an off-white material was chosen. Perhaps you will be surprised to find praying hands in the corner. We pray that Watergate has been a lesson for all Americans. The straight and narrow way is the best. Within minutes of the President's speech, the resignation date was being stitched on the quilt. The quilt is bound in gauze. Just trying to heal the wounds."

I don't know what Mrs. Guthrie has added to or subtracted from the quilt since I saw it in the fall of 1976, but there is no doubt she has made a stark and pertinent statement of the times.

Appliqué quilt, "Octagonal Flower Garden," designed by Marian Wittenberg, art teacher in John F. Kennedy High School, Somers, New York. Quilt appliquéd and quilted by senior high girls as a class project. Their signatures are embroidered in octagonal blocks. Photo, courtesy Marian Wittenberg.

No less relevant, and certainly of equal importance, is the "Prosperity Is Just Around the Corner" quilt made by Fannie B. Shaw of Texas. Again, she tells the story of her quilt:

"During the Depression we lived in the country. We had everything we wanted (but money), we raised cows, hogs, chickens, turkeys, cotton, corn, had a team of mules. The depression didn't hurt us at all, but the boys from the cities and thousands of country boys were the ones that seem to be hurt most.

"They were walking the streets and roads looking for work. We took in 4 boys from dif. states and dif. times. So touching to hear they had walked holes in their shoes, went hungry, slept on the road side at night. All day & night the radio would repeat Hoover's words 'Prosperity is just around the corner.' I began to think 'I wish I could paint a picture to bring to life those words'. It was on my mind so strong—so one night I had something like a premonition, about how it would look on Cloth. Determination struck also. So I got everything ready to begin putting my feelings on cloth. I made the house wife & farmer first. So they looked

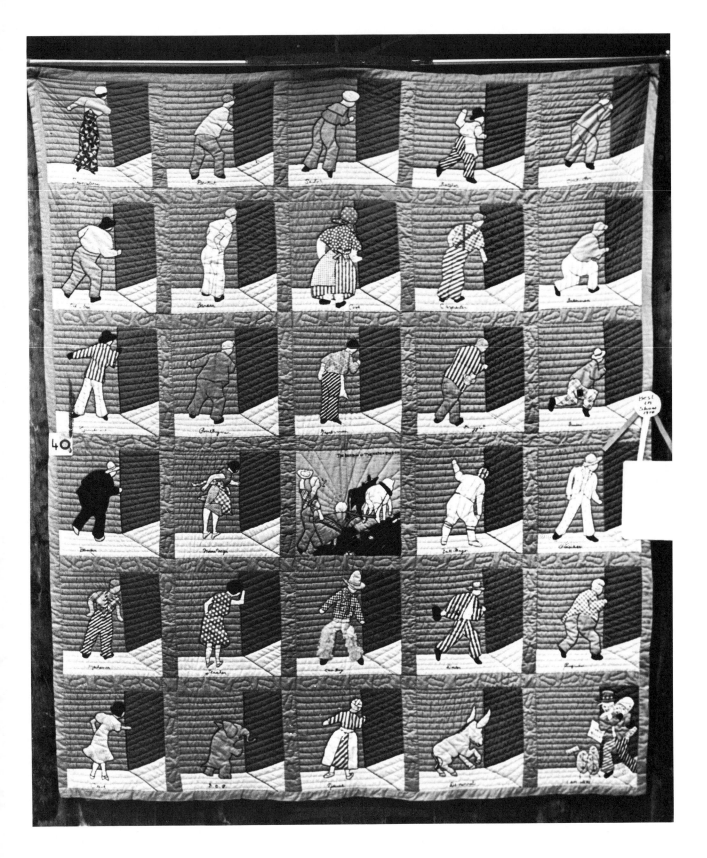

perfect. I knew I had started right, from there I kept going 4 mo. 10 mo. 18 mo. then I was ready to set the blocks together with strips—then is when I rem. about the foot steps the boys had talked about walking all day. So I quilted the foot prints between each block leading in all directions. The Country boys were going to town looking for jobs, City boys coming to the Country, going from one family to another willing to work for what they eat. Though we paid them what the farm wages were. They all went away with new clothes and some money.

"There are over 1100 pieces in the quilt. Took me about 2 mo. to quilt it. All these people from all walks of life are peeping around the corner for better time."

And all of them were—Fannie B. Shaw has pictured the farmer, housewife, banker, seamstress, cook, doctor, preacher, bum, cowboy, ball player, butcher, conductor, GOP elephant, Democratic donkey, nurse, clerk, teacher, merchant, baker, sailor, dentist, oil-gas man, lumberman, poultryman, grocer, druggist, mechanic, engineer, and Uncle Sam.

Such abstraction of reality as these two quilts represent may be possible in academic art; here, the quilt maker has raised fabric interpretation to the highest possible level in historical imagery. The craving to express ourselves creatively in quilt making, in other forms of appliqué, or in other types of crafts is encouraging and enlightening; we learn who the people are by what they do. Creative necessity is a force to be reckoned with.

Opposite: **"Prosperity Is Just Around the Corner," designed and made by Fannie B. Shaw. This quilt took "Best in Show" at the Texas Quilt Show. The story of the quilt appears in the text on pages 95 and 97. Photo, Lee Langum.**

12

"I HAVE DECKED MY BED WITH COVERINGS OF TAPESTRY" (PROVERBS):

More Quilts

There are, of course, many kinds of appliqué quilts, but it is easier just now for us to divide them into two categories—traditional and pictorial.

Most of the traditional patterns are florals; their design is stylized, formally arranged, and repetitive. Order and balance characterize the design. Many of these floral patterns—or variations of them—are available now in pattern books or magazines, or can be sketched from photographs. Although these old patterns have been used hundreds of times by hundreds of women, and probably will continue to be, the pattern you select can wear the stamp of your individuality by the treatment or approach you take.

For instance, most of the backgrounds of the antique appliqué quilts were white or unbleached, occasionally a soft pastel. Why not reverse this and use a deep, rich color—an earthy brown, a navy blue, a smoky gray, or brick red—as the background? Also, try reversing the appliqué designs—use solids where prints and calicoes have been used most often in the past; increase the size of the blooms, or try a different set. Remember, however, that the *type* of fabric is of great importance in making a quilt—you'll eventually be quilting your masterpiece, so pay attention to the material. Use a lightweight or dress-weight fabric, 100 percent cotton where possible, in broadcloth or percale. The all-cotton fabric will make sewing immeasurably easier for appliqué work; if you must use a poly-cotton blend, try to keep it for the background.

This type of appliqué quilt is usually made for the bed and not the wall, so here are some things for you to think about, some decisions to make.

TRADITIONAL APPLIQUÉ QUILT

1. Choose your pattern.
2. Decide on the size of the quilt—twin, double, etc.
3. Choose color scheme and fabrics, for both background and appliqué, also for backing and binding.
4. Decide on the set, or design. This is important, for it determines not only the size of the block but the number of blocks you will need. For instance, you'll need a lot more 33-cm (13-in.) blocks to cover a given area than if you were using 46-cm (18-in.) blocks. If you sew the blocks together edge to edge when you're finished, it will take twice as many appliquéd blocks as it would if

you alternated them with solid or plain blocks. You can also separate the blocks by strips or sashes; you can join four to six blocks together to make a center medallion, surround it with two or three different borders, then add another row of appliqué blocks. In fact, there are so many choices in a quilt set that it's worthwhile to give it a lot of thought.

5. Make a sample block of the pattern you've chosen. Not only is this block a reference guide, but you'll find out if the pattern goes together easily and if you enjoy working on it. Make the

Four traditional appliqué quilt designs. Diagonal lines represent finger-pressed lines or thread basting for help in accurate placement on foundation block. a. "Bridal wreath." b. "Prairie flower." c. "Hearts and flowers." d. "Tulip."

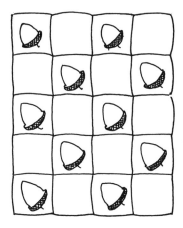

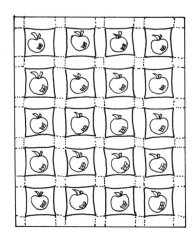

Right: Quilt set showing appliquéd blocks joined edge to edge with alternating plain or solid squares.

Far right: Quilt set with strips or sashing between the appliquéd blocks. Corner squares on strips, shown by dotted lines, could be a different color than strips.

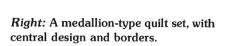

Right: A medallion-type quilt set, with central design and borders.

Far right: Overlapping strips add an unusual touch to a diagonal medallion.

sample before you buy any quantity of fabric in case you change your mind about color and pattern.

6. Trace pattern pieces on thin cardboard or fine sandpaper, and, since this is appliqué, *include a 6-mm (¼-in.) seam allowance.* Make several duplicates of the pattern; cardboard especially wears on the edges and needs to be replaced after several uses.

7. Consider using commercial bias tape for floral stems, wreaths, or circles.

8. Cut background blocks from chosen fabric; be accurate in cutting, and include the seam allowance, for eventually all such blocks must come together in a neat four-square way.

9. Transfer the complete appliqué design to the background fabric. This is as important in a repetitive design as it is in most pictorial designs. You've got to come out even with balance and form, and guesswork won't do it for you. A lopsided flower or misplaced wreath can be a constant reproach to you. There are two easy ways to make everything come out neat and tidy— discussed earlier in the section on transferring design, but I'll refresh your memory.

 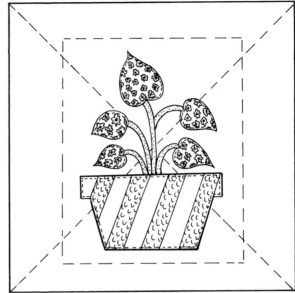

The first method is a stencil. Cut a square from cardboard or poster board the exact size of your background block, including seam allowance. Center your design on this and trace around it. Now put the cardboard on a thick magazine or bread board and pin or thumbtack it in place so it won't slip. Use a single-edge razor blade or Exacto knife to cut out the appliqué design; the part that's left is the stencil. Place it on each background fabric square and outline the cutout shapes with a pencil.

The second method is the light box or light method. If you have bought or made a light box, fine, use it; you can also use a window in daylight. Remember to trace your pattern on paper instead of cardboard; go over the markings so they are dark and distinct and will show up; tape the fabric in place over the paper, let the light shine through, and go on with the transferring.

10. Trace your master pattern again on thin cardboard, but this time cut the pattern apart for use with appliqué shapes. When you repeat several shapes in a design—for instance, four tulips or four roses—try cutting four layers of fabric at once. Stack the fabric carefully and pin the layers together. Place the cardboard template on the fabric; it is important to remember that bias can work to your advantage in appliqué work. The edges are easier to turn under, so lay the pattern on the fabric accordingly. Add a little seam allowance as you cut; you must be sure to cover the marking lines on the background, and this will keep all of your designs uniform. If you cut more than one layer of fabric at a time, only the top layer will have the design outline traced inside the seam allowance. However, this is not a problem; remember that a standard seam allowance is 6 mm (¼ in.); cut out fabric pieces carefully, turn under the raw edges, baste in place, and you

Two drawings that show the importance of accurate design placement on background. First is off-center and unbalanced, definitely incorrect; second is placed correctly. Dotted diagonal lines show finger creases or thread basting to help in placement.

Above: "The Watermelon Patch," appliquéd quilt designed and made by Dawn Beecher. A rousing, good-time, old-fashioned watermelon feast brought to life in fabric. Photo, Susie Montgomery.

Right: "A Rose Is a Rose Is a Rose," by the author. A crib-size quilt, made of six blocks of variations of traditional rose appliqué patterns, in shades of rose, pink, and red on a pale gray cotton ground. Hand sewn, hand quilted. Photo, Stubby Crowe.

should come out even. You can use less turn-under than this if you want to; remember to keep even measurements so that the design will fit easily to the background square.

PICTORIAL OR PERSONAL APPLIQUÉ QUILTS

There is much more freedom of expression in this type of quilt, and you can set your own pace. For instance, the background blocks don't all have to be the same color, and they don't have to be the same size. Often you need not plan the quilt set ahead, but work it out as you go along. You might have a central theme—for instance, your family life. A simple appliqué of your house could be a center medallion, surrounded by fabric pictures of daily living—children, pets, the family car, the telephone, the traffic sign, the school bus, and the church.

You might want to record a special event in a quilt—a vacation trip or other family outings. If you're a nature lover, you might want to appliqué various trees and leaves, flowers or birds, or your own garden. When you've decided, make a rough sketch of

Monopoly Quilt by Dawn Beecher. A bed-size playing board for the game "Monopoly," entirely hand sewn. Some letters are appliquéd but most are hand embroidered in satin stitch. Game board has a filler of polyester batting and is hand quilted. Border and backing are of blue velveteen. Photo, Stubby Crowe.

each block. If you need accurately defined patterns for working, then refine your sketch into a detailed drawing; trace it on other paper or cardboard, and cut the tracing into pattern pieces. Small details can easily be worked in embroidery.

These personal quilts are easy and pleasant to work on. You can add blocks as you get ideas for them, and when you have finished enough for a quilt, spread them out on the floor and see how they fit together. Move the blocks around until you are happy with the way they look; strips of fabric can be added to any of the blocks to make them fit neatly into a section.

Whether you are making a full-size or crib-size, wall-size or doll-size quilt, once the blocks or sections are appliquéd, you're ready to decide on the quilting. Most pictorial designs are quilted in contour, but no rule says it must be this way. Acquaint yourself with the choices, then make up your mind.

13

YOU GO YOUR WAY, I'LL GO MINE:

Ways to Quilt

There are both practical and aesthetic reasons for quilting. When you quilt something, it is warmer—two or three layers are warmer than one. You add more than warmth with quilting, however; you add an extra dimension that creates a textural interest. There is a play of light against dark. The little shadows cast by the tiny ridges and channels made by quilting lines add depth to surface decoration. *What* you're quilting often answers the question of *how* you will quilt it—by hand or machine, or a combination of both. The effects are different. With machine quilting or stitching, the quilting lines are solid and unbroken. When you quilt by hand, there is a space between each stitch and the effect is of a broken or dotted line.

The size of your project also affects your decision. It is very difficult to quilt a bed-size quilt by machine, for sheer bulk makes it hard to handle. Also, most quilt makers and quilt lovers take a dim view of machine quilting; I've seen some beautiful examples, and I've often wondered how the quilt makers managed, especially if the quilting design has curves or circles in it. There is scarcely room under the head of the machine for even a snugly rolled quilt to rest. We've already talked about quilting smaller or other projects than bed quilts—machine quilting can be very effective when used on wall hangings, banners, pillows, or garments. Most of these articles are smaller than quilts, but when working even with a very large hanging, you *can* juggle it in place under the presser foot, and sometimes you can quilt in sections, then join the sections later.

Quilting small articles is fairly easy, but since we've been talking about bed-size quilts, here are some suggestions for you to consider before you start your quilting—hand quilting, that is. Probably the essentials are already in your sewing basket or pocket waiting for you. You need quilting thread; this is slightly heavier than regular sewing thread and is coated lightly with silicone so it will slide easily in and out of the fabric layers. Quilting thread comes in many colors; it does not come in black. If you can't find quilting thread, use heavy-duty or mercerized thread coated with beeswax. After you thread the needle, just run the thread through one of those little slots in the plastic case, and that will do the trick. You can buy regular quilting needles, too. Sometimes they are called "betweens"; a size 7 or 8 works very well—it depends a lot on your eyesight. Also, you need a thimble. You may fuss and fume about this, for at first they are awkward and hard to get used to, but it is worth a little practice and determination if you don't want a perforated middle finger the rest of your life.

The quilting stitch is a running stitch; I can feel the purists bristle with claims that the true quilting stitch is one at a time, the needle pushed perpendicularly through the layers with the right hand, received underneath with the left, and pushed back up through to the top to be then received by the right hand (or reversed, if you're left-handed). Anyway, I use a running stitch and most of the quilters I know use it, too. You hold the needle between your thumb and first finger, at an acute angle to the quilt; your thimble finger rests on the heel of the needle, ready to push. After a few tries, you'll be able to get two or three stitches on your needle before you come up for air.

The assembly of the quilt is basically the same whether you plan to quilt each block or strip separately, or join all blocks and sections together before you start to quilt. In either case, you have the appliquéd top, the middle layer (which is usually polyester batting), and the lining or backing layer. If you are quilting block by block, or if you have joined together several blocks in a strip, the backing and batting are cut the same size as the top sections. When you are working with a completed quilt top with all blocks joined before quilting, then cut the backing 5 to 7.5 cm (2 to 3 in.) larger all the way around. This provides an easy way to bind off the edges of the finished quilt. Bring the backing over the raw edges to the face side of the quilt; decide how wide the binding is to be, trim the extra fabric, turn under the 6-mm (¼-in.) seam allowance, and whip the backing to the top of the quilt. This makes a nice, neat binding.

In stacking your quilt layers, start with the backing; place it right side *down* against a flat surface. This might be the floor if you are working with a whole quilt top; it could be a card table if you're working with a single section. Next comes the layer of batting; smooth it out and line up the sides and corners. Now comes the final layer, the appliquéd block or top, design *up*. Pin in place, keeping the layers smooth. A whole quilt is difficult to pin because it is so large; invite a friend to help. Begin to pin from the center out; on a large quilt, you may have to crawl (carefully, with shoes off) to the center, then pin with one hand, since you can't get the other hand underneath the quilt. After the pinning is done, it's a good idea to thread-baste to keep all the layers in place. Some of my quilting friends don't do this, but it gives me a sense of security, and it keeps my quilting thread from catching on pins.

Before you begin to quilt, you must decide on a quilting pattern. You don't want to overwhelm your appliqué design with quilting, and usually outline or contour quilting works very well; also, it doesn't necessitate marking quilting lines. You simply follow the outline of the appliqué, then quilt successive lines 6 mm to 1.3 cm (¼ to ½ in.) apart. If you prefer to fill in the background with a diagonal or square grid, use a ruler to keep the lines straight. You can pencil them in lightly, or you can use masking tape. The tape works very well—lay it alongside the ruler, and press it gently to the fabric. Quilt on both sides of it, then peel it off, and use it again.

If your quilt has strips between the blocks, or the appliquéd blocks are separated by plain ones, or you have borders, you may want to use a more elaborate quilting design. You could choose any of the traditional patterns that are available in books or magazines or from mail-order needlework houses, or you can draw your own. Many of these patterns are perforated; place the pattern over the block to be marked, rub powdered chalk through the holes with a little wad of cotton, then lift off the pattern. The chalk marks will stay long enough for you to quilt the design, but mark each section this way as you come to it; otherwise the chalk will disappear before you get to it.

You're right! There *are* a lot of things to think about, a lot of decisions to make, when you tackle a large quilt, but getting there is half the fun. If you've decided to join blocks and complete the top before quilting, then you must also decide whether to quilt with or without a frame.

QUILTING THE WHOLE QUILT ON A FRAME

This is a traditional method of quilting, one that is still popular because of the tension it provides. Frames require a lot of room, although this may not be a problem for you. When your quilt is assembled and ready to put in the frame, baste each end of the quilt securely to the fabric apron tacked or stapled to each long roller. Now roll one end of the quilt *under* on the roller until only 46 to 51 cm (18 to 20 in.) are left exposed. Next, fasten the shorter rail or side pieces—or stretchers, whatever you wish to call them—to the rollers. Depending on the kind of frame you have, you'll use C clamps, pegs, or notches or tighten them with a ratchet. You're ready now to quilt the exposed section. When this is finished, remove the side pieces and roll the quilted area *under* on the top roller, thus exposing a new area to be quilted. Attach the side pieces again to the rollers, and get back to work. Continue in this manner until the entire quilt has been quilted, then remove it from the frame.

QUILTING A WHOLE QUILT WITHOUT A FRAME

This requires a great deal of basting, so be prepared. You'll be handling the quilt all the time, and you must keep those layers together smoothly; otherwise you'll have wrinkles and pleats on the back—maybe the front, too—when you finish. It's very comfy to quilt on a cold winter's night with a quilt spread over your knees, but you can also use the dining room table or the ironing board. If it is too cumbersome to spread the quilt out, then roll it up, anchor the roll with safety pins, and leave an exposed strip

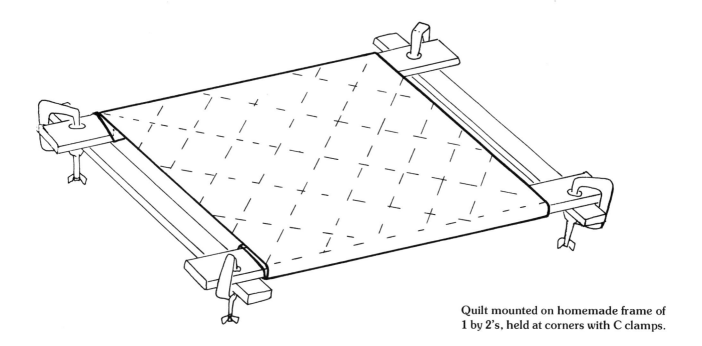

Quilt mounted on homemade frame of 1 by 2's, held at corners with C clamps.

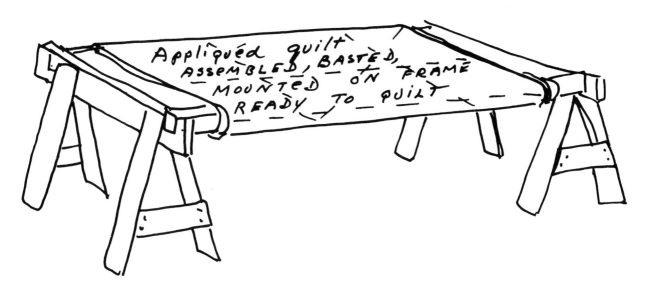

Appliquéd quilt assembled, basted, mounted on frame ready to quilt

Quilt mounted on floor frame, ready for quilting.

hanging over the edge of the table or ironing board. Pull up a chair and start in.

QUILTING WITH A HOOP

Large, oval quilting hoops that come with floor standards (removable) are sturdy enough to handle a full-size quilt. The hoop, like an embroidery hoop, consists of two wooden rings fitted together. The outer ring has a clamp on it. Lay the quilt over the inside ring; loosen the clamp so the outer ring will fit over the quilt, then tighten the clamp until the two rings hold the quilt snugly between them. You can remove the hoop from the floor standard and do your quilting on a tabletop if you prefer. Once you've quilted the area inside the hoop, move the rings to the next section and keep on going.

PIECEMEAL QUILTING

Some people would like to make a quilt but are staggered at the thought of such a large project. It's nice to know you can quilt in bits and pieces. Some call this quilting block by block, or quilting as you go. It boils down to the fact that you quilt each block separately, then join them together afterward. If the blocks are small, you can join several together in strips or sections, do the quilting, then join these together later. One of the great advantages, and to me, a great joy, is that quilting this way makes everything portable. You *can* take it with you. Also, when all the sections are finally joined together into a full-size quilt, no one will be able to tell by looking at it what method you used. Only the back will be different. The seams joining the blocks or strips will show, but they create their own patchwork design, and absolutely no rule says your backing has to be one large piece of fabric.

When you are quilting this way, you don't cut the backing larger than the top; both batting and backing are cut the same size and stacked together as described earlier. The most important thing to remember is that you must stop quilting 1.3 cm (½ in.) from the edges of the block so that the layers will be free for seaming together. If the set of your quilt calls for sashing or strips between the appliquéd blocks, add the strips to the block before assembling the layers. For instance, suppose your block measures 33 cm (13 in.); you want to add a 5-cm (2-in.) strip to separate the blocks. Cut the strips and seam them to the blocks as in the diagram, since one strip only is needed between two blocks. This added strip will give you a 38-cm (15-in.) square for most of the quilt—the blocks along one side will be rectangular instead of square, since there must be a final strip to balance the whole. After you've joined the sashing strips to each block, *then* cut batting and backing pieces and go ahead with quilting; this eliminates any sashing strips from the back of the quilt.

QUILTING—STARTING AND STOPPING

You already know about quilting thread, needles, and stitches, and now you need to know how to start and how to stop.

There are two methods for starting. In the first one, knot the thread. Bring needle up from backing through to top or face of quilt. When you feel the knot tight against the backing, give the thread a little tug; you'll hear a "pop," and the knot will go through the backing and get lost in the middle layer.

The second method of starting is from the top of the quilt instead of underneath—no knot this time. Insert needle on the

Appliquéd quilt blocks showing additions of strips before blocks are quilted separately or in sections. See also joining instructions below.

line to be quilted, about 2.5 cm (1 in.) *below* the starting point. Slide the needle through the *middle layer only* and emerge at the place where you want to begin quilting. Pull thread gently until the end of it barely disappears, then start to quilt. You're headed down to where you first inserted the needle, so that your first stitches will catch the end of the thread and secure it. If you're worried about it catching, after a few stitches, tug lightly on the thread; if it doesn't pull out, everything is fine and you can keep on going. Otherwise, you'll have to start again, but after a little practice, there won't be a problem.

You don't want a knot to show when you start quilting, and you certainly don't want one to show when you stop. When you are ready for the last quilting stitch on a line, make a tiny knot in the thread. Hold the needle close to the fabric, throw the thread over the needle, and pull the needle through the loop. This little knot will disappear as you take the last stitch; go back over the last stitch, through the same hole, but don't go through all three layers. Slide the needle through the middle layer only, then bring it out a little distance away through the top. Pull up slightly on the thread and clip it; the end will sink back underneath, and no one will know where you started quilting or where you stopped. And that's our aim.

When you have quilted the blocks or sections, you are ready to join them together. For this, you'll use that 1.3-cm (½-in.) space you left unquilted all around the outside edge.

JOINING QUILTED BLOCKS

Working on a flat surface, put two quilted blocks or strips together, *right sides touching.* Line up edges and corners so that they meet properly. Fold back the batting and backing and pin so

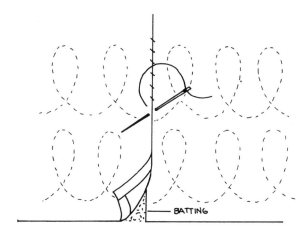

Joining prequilted blocks or sections. Drawing shows quilt from backing side, with one raw edge turned under and sewed to backing of adjoining block.

BATTING

they'll stay out of your way; you will seam *only* through the tops or face of your blocks. This seam will be 6 mm (¼ in.) wide, which is fairly standard for this. When you've stitched the seam, open the blocks face down on the table and smooth them out. You may have to trim the edges of the batting a little; you want the batting to butt, not overlap. Now, smooth one backing piece over the batting; fold under 6 mm (¼ in.) along the edge of the other backing section, place the folded edge over the raw edge of the first block, and whip- or slip-stitch in place. Join all blocks, sections, or strips together in this manner.

FINISHING OR BINDING THE EDGES OF THE QUILT

This is the last step. We've already mentioned one method of handling this. Cut the backing large enough to use for binding or border, and when the quilting is finished, bring this backing forward to the face of the quilt, turn under the raw edge, and pin, then sew in place.

For a separate binding, you can cut strips of fabric either on straight of grain or on bias. Cutting your own bias takes a lot of fabric, and you can buy 2.5-cm (1-in.) commercial bias binding in many colors; it comes with edges turned under and pressed. This works well for a single binding.

For double binding, cut the strips twice the finished width plus seam allowances. For instance, if the finished width of the binding is to be 1.3 cm (½ in.), cut a strip 3.8 cm (1½ in.) wide. Fold strip lengthwise, wrong sides together, and press. Baste raw edges together, or pin at intervals. Line up raw edges of binding evenly against raw edges of quilt along the backing side; stitch in place through all layers. Now bring the folded edge of the binding forward over the seamed edges, and whip in place, covering all raw edges.

All of the techniques described here are primarily for use in quilt making, no matter what size, but you can also use them for many other articles. Methods of quilting and binding or finishing are basically the same for home decorative projects, small gift items, or articles of clothing.

Banners and hangings are as closely associated with appliqué as the word *hand* is with *glove*. The history of banners is a long one, but we can't quite place the beginnings. They are mentioned often in the Bible; they were used—and still are—in Egypt and India. Cloth banners very possibly originated in Rome, an outgrowth of heavy metal standards used in military conquests. The cross was one of the first symbols used on banners and appeared during the fourth century when Constantine ruled. Today, use of the cross is widespread; it appears in many variations on flags and banners of European countries—Finland, Denmark, and Greece are three—as well as state flags of America; Alabama, Hawaii, and Florida are thus represented. Perhaps the best-known banner cross of all, however, is that which appears on the International Red Cross flag.

We associate banners with ecclesiastical processions and purpose, for they have played a major role in such ceremonies for centuries. They are rich in symbolism and bold of design; today, they are still carried in processions, and whether indoors or out, they dazzle the eye and warm the spirit. They played an important role during the Crusades of the Middle Ages. Those were the times of suits of armor and closed helmets, and believe me, it was important to know who was hiding behind all that metal! Earlier battle standards were rigid and heavy and certainly hard to handle while riding a horse; thus, in time, pieces of cloth were substituted. These were simple—colored strips fastened to a staff—but readily visible at a distance. At least it became possible to distinguish friend from foe, and often it meant one could get back to the castle for a hot meal and a good night's sleep instead of becoming a casualty statistic.

Banners have always had a role to play. They were invented to identify, to inform, or both. They still do. We see them now suspended over a busy street with traffic snarled below, inviting us to come to the fair, the races, or the bazaar. Hung from facades and shop windows, they advertise articles and merchandise sold within. Hung from museums and galleries, they beckon us inside. Drenched in color, they move constantly, caught in the lightest breeze, floating in the air, and it is this very motion that plays an integral part in attracting our attention. They have an air of gaiety about them, an air of abandon, and there is a joyous quality even to the ones carried in religious processions.

14

RALLY 'ROUND THE FLAG, BOYS!

Banners and Hangings

A welcome banner to be hung in a doorway or as a room divider. Since the complete banner consists of five separate sections, you could make interchangeable units for use at holiday times or for special celebrations.

Banners are used inside today as often as they are outside, and many people consider banners and hangings interchangeable. Perhaps there is no clear delineation, except that a dominant characteristic of a banner is that it is suspended from above and hangs free. A hanging *could* be mounted on a frame and still be called a hanging, but a banner never could. Both can be lined and/or quilted, although again, we associate banners with a single layer of cloth; for some reason, we think of hangings as more permanent, though this is not necessarily so. Both have the medium of appliqué in common; both employ the same elements of design, often the same fabrics and techniques, the same embellishments, the same finishings, so they most certainly are kissing cousins. I tend to argue with some of the definitions—a hanging in or on a frame becomes a picture as far as I am concerned, and if you hang a banner at right angles to a staff, it's no longer a banner, but a flag.

What you call them is up to you. They can hang on a wall, from the ceiling, in a doorway, over open shelves or closets; they can

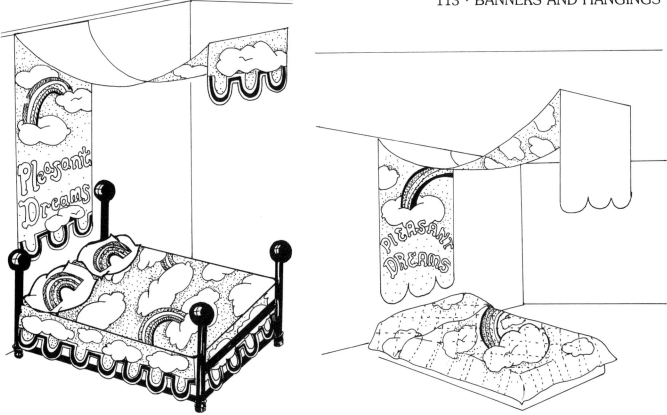

be used to celebrate the seasons or family happenings; you can put pockets on them and use them for storage in the kitchen, the bathroom, a bedroom, or a child's room. You can make them by hand or machine to fit any occasion; they can be rolled up for easy storage and transportation. Like slipcovers, they can be used as instant decorating and give your house or apartment a whole new look.

I remember the World's Fair held in New York several years ago. I went into the Vatican Pavilion and saw the entire place ablaze with Norman LaLiberté's banners. He drew on biblical themes for his designs; they were vigorous, almost primitive in feeling, but bold and simple, and they dominated the room. LaLiberté raised banner making to a new high; today his work is greatly in demand, and graces many private offices and public buildings. He pioneered in new forms of banner making, and since then, many people have been enchanted with the magic of making them.

The basic techniques of appliqué detailed in earlier chapters apply to making banners and hangings as well as other forms of appliqué, but the following information will undoubtedly be helpful to you.

1. Banners can be made by an individual, or made by

Above left: **A bed banner or a canopy planned to fit in wall space at head of bed. Design carries out theme of bedspread or quilt.**

Above right: **Another canopy, this time for a casual sleeping arrangement—a mattress or pad on the floor. Canopies such as these actually can be any length—shortened to fit the wall space immediately above the head of the bed, or somewhat longer to extend to ceiling and cover pillow space. One could be the length of the bed as shown here, or lengthened so that the final drop comes to the foot of the bed, thus enclosing it at top and bottom.**

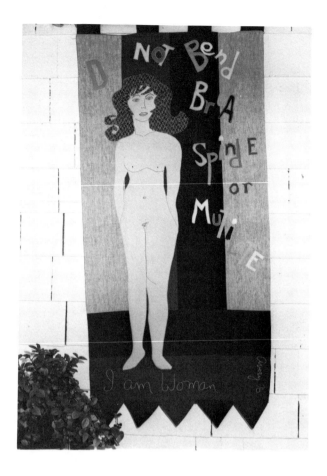

Above: "I Am Woman" by the author. Felt figure and letters machine appliquéd to a striped Mexican cotton. Idea from the stern admonition on monthly bills—"Do not bend, break, spindle, or mutilate." Photo, Stubby Crowe.

Above right: Large wall hanging by Jody Schnautz. Reverse appliqué, with some regular appliqué used; medium- to heavy-weight fabrics in purples, orange, and green. Random-size blocks joined together and lined. Hanging was designed and worked in one of author's classes. Photo, Stubby Crowe.

groups—such as churches, clubs, and schools. Hangings are made usually only by an individual.

2. Banners can hang outdoors as well as in. Hangings are for the inside.

3. Banners primarily communicate; they have a message, proclamation, or direction; thus letters, numbers, signs, and symbols are commonly used as subject matter. Hangings may include these, but they are not limited to communication.

4. Decide on the purpose of your banner or hanging; its ultimate use will determine form, fabric, and design. If a banner is for outdoors, think of using a nylon rainproof material or a "wash and wear" polyester blend. Also, if it is to be an outdoor banner, will it hang like a flag from a staff, be hung against a building, or carried suspended from a standard? Whatever your choice of fabric, it should be heavy enough to hang well and support the appliqué design, even if it means adding a lining.

If the banner or hanging is for the inside, measure the space and use it as a guide for size.

5. Sketch your design full scale; tape shelf or brown wrapping paper together if you do not have other paper large enough. The time may well come when you do not need or want a preliminary

sketch but can "draw" with your scissors; until then, you're safer with a plan. If you are using letters or numbers, cut them from colored construction paper and move them around on the drawing until you are happy with the placement; you can use the cutouts as patterns later. Felt pens or crayons can be used too, and the color combinations will help you with design.

6. Select your fabrics. Good background or foundation fabrics are upholstery materials, wools, heavy cottons, velveteen and velvets, lightweight canvas, linens, and twills. Burlap, although inexpensive, shouldn't be used for anything you want to last for a while; it fades, and it stretches. Don't forget felt; I have a high regard for it and think it has been greatly underrated. The techniques of making felt go back to nomadic tribes long before the birth of Christ. It was used extensively in religious and royal ceremonies in preference to silk. I read only recently that Genghis Khan was crowned with felt. Today it is so widely used in many fields—clothing, home accessories, interior decoration—that it is difficult to list them all. The heavier felts are excellent for foundation use, and the lighter weights for appliqué shapes. It also has the built-in advantage that you don't have to bother turning under the edges.

Your foundation material does not have to be in one large piece for either a banner or wall hanging. It can consist of smaller

Above: A banner for the beach. Cover a 6-foot strip of 1-inch-thick foam rubber with appliquéd fabric; measure and stitch ties in place. When rolled up and tied, this banner goes to the beach for comfortable sitting or sunbathing; when not in use, beach roll can hang on wall in playroom or den for storage and still be part of the decor.

Left: "St. Francis," appliqué picture by the author. Embroiderers' Guild design. Hand appliquéd of felt, wool, and cotton on gray denim ground; embroidered details. From the collection of Dr. and Mrs. Joseph Bishop. Photo, Stubby Crowe.

Above: A banner using hands as a design element; this one, "Family Hands," with tracings of hands from children to grandparents. Machine appliquéd on heavy denim; stuffed, quilted, and finished with yarn tassels. Photo, Stubby Crowe.

Right: "Hillsdale Hands," a felt "friendship" banner appliquéd with hands cut from various cotton fabrics. Embroidered names; machine appliqué; bottom edge finished with ball fringe. Felt by Continental Felt. Photo, Stubby Crowe.

Both banners designed and made by the author.

sections sewed together, in much the same manner as you would sew a patchwork quilt. You can seam the patches or sections if you are working with woven fabrics and have to deal with raw edges. If working with felt, fit the pieces together like a jigsaw puzzle and sew them one at a time to the ground fabric with the edges butted together.

7. For appliqué shapes, you can use almost anything; refer to the fabric listing at the beginning of the book.

8. Stitch by hand or machine or a combination of both. Add stitchery if you like, and any other "found" objects or extras—beads, shells, or feathers, for example.

9. For hanging your work, tabs or a casing are easiest and most satisfactory. Decide how many tabs, what size, and how close together you want them. The size of the rod or pole will help determine the size, too. Tabs can be made of felt, of background fabric, or of one of the appliqué fabrics; they can be plain or appliquéd. You can use ribbon or braid and fasten the tabs with buttons or beads instead of sewing them in place. You can also make buttonholes or eyelets across the top and lace rope or cord through them for hanging.

"Old-Fashioned Lady" by Margaret Cusack. An appliqué picture with a distinct air of nostalgia about it. A brooch is pinned on the delicate white fabric of the high collar; the lady's dress is shown using right and wrong sides of fabrics to portray trimming and folds; it appears as companion prints. There are real buttons on the front of her dress; note the shadows on face and hands portrayed in different fabric. Background is large floral-patterned brocade. Photo, courtesy Margaret Cusack.

"Marilyn," appliquéd portrait of Marilyn Monroe by Margaret Cusack. Earrings are rhinestones, face is satin, hair is satin and corduroy. Rose-colored satin background with stars appliquéd. Size, 1¼ meters (4 feet) square. Photo, courtesy Margaret Cusack.

A game banner. This is a game for blindfolded players, one of whom must mend the lady's broken heart by pinning a whole heart in its place. Hearts are of felt and are kept in the pocket stitched on lower right side of banner. A variation of this game could be to use "bean-bag" hearts; put banner on floor, then toss hearts and try to get one in the right place.

Fold edge over & stitch down to hold dowel

Cut the top of banner in turrets, scallops, or v's, turn over & stitch in place.

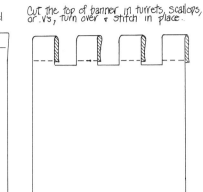

Far left: Banner or hanging with top hem folded over to back, ready to stitch for casing.

Left: Top of banner cut out in turret shapes, turned over, and stitched to make loops for hanging.

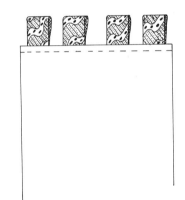

Decorative tapes, ribbons, or strips of fabric can also be used as loops. Here they are stitched on the front *(left)* and back *(right)*.

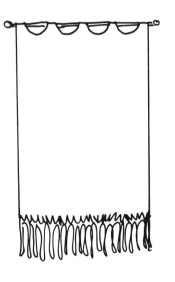

Another way to make loops. Circles are cut out and edges bound at top of banner; banner is then folded to back along dotted line and stitched in place. Circles make scalloped loops for dowel or rod.

10. Lining the banner or hanging: cut lining fabric the same length as the project, but about 2.5 cm (1 in.) narrower. Press, if necessary. Put lining against banner, right sides together, and pin both side edges together, then stitch each side. At this stage it is a good idea to turn the banner to the right side and press the seam. This will also establish a pressed side edge; the lining, since it was cut smaller, will not come quite to the edge and the seam will be along the back. Now turn wrong side out again. If you are using tabs, line them up across the top and machine-baste in place; the raw edges of the tabs will be even with the top raw edge of the banner. If it is easier to do this step before you do any sewing on the lining, then do this first and get it out of the way. After machine basting the tabs, place lining over them and pin across top; turn banner over so you can see the machine-basting line. Use that line as a guide, and stitch just underneath it from side edge to side edge, across the top. Turn, press, and finish the bottom of the lining by hand.

Strips of fabric stitched around sides of banner or hanging to make a border. Fabric strip is stitched to top of banner, right sides together. Next step is to turn strip to the back, leaving a border, and tack down along seam in the back.
Below right: **Finished border at top and sides.**

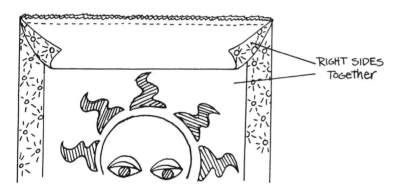

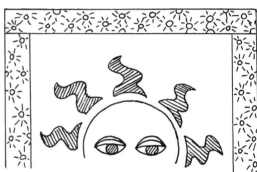

RIGHT SIDES Together

A banner finish; raw edges are turned under on all sides, pressed, and stitched. Separate loops can be added, or a casing stitched on by hand along the back.

Left: Edges of banner finished with self-fringe, made by pulling out threads along raw edges. Top line of fringe can be replaced with loops or casing. If left, as shown in drawing, stitch casing by hand along top edge on wrong side of banner.

Below: Steps in mitering a corner for a border on a wall hanging or banner. The finished banner is shown in *d.*

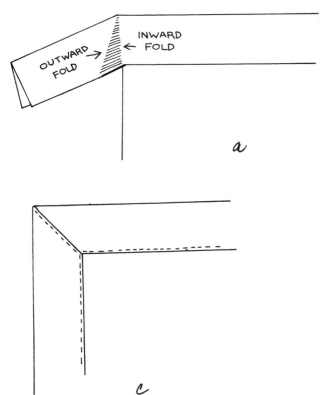

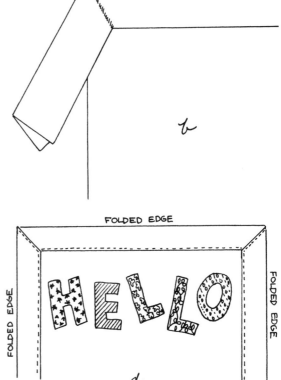

Above: Rockefeller Center Banner, 1.5 by 2.6 meters (5 by 8 feet). This stunning banner is a tribute to group effort. It was made by seventy-five children and adults from New York's five boroughs, as a celebration for the city in the Bicentennial year. Following a tour of Rockefeller Center, banner workshop members documented the various buildings, sculptures, and gardens, under instructor Sally Pleet of Community Environments. Photo, courtesy Sally Pleet.

Right: Appliqué hanging, "Godey Ladies," by Gladys Boalt. Background is cream, with soft pale green foreground. Hanging was drawn in detail before being transferred to fabric. Faces and clothing details are hand embroidered. All hand appliquéd and hand quilted in close contour pattern. Border is brown, with machine embroidery at top edge, hand embroidery on the bottom. Size, approximately 50 by 65 cm (20½ by 27 in.). Photo, Stubby Crowe.

11. Wall hangings are usually a little more formal than banners and consequently would be finished straight across the bottom edge. With banners, you can let yourself go, with beads, tassels, scallops, fringe, bells, or anything your fancy dictates. Most banners and hangings are smaller than quilts and thus take less time to make. Even if you'd like to make a quilt eventually, it's a good idea to start on a smaller scale. You have unlimited subject matter in banners and hangings; they can adorn your house, embellish your walls, amuse your family or friends, provoke a conversation,

Above, left and right: Banners hanging in the Rye, New York, Presbyterian Church, made by young people of the congregation. Felt, cotton, and burlap. Photos, Stubby Crowe.

"Hearts and Flowers" banner, made by a sixth-grade class from P.S. 193, Queens, New York. Sally Pleet, of Community Environments, was instructor. Size, 1.75 meters (5½ feet) square. Each of the fifty state flowers is reproduced in the big center heart, and New York is represented by the lone rose. Of felt, in various bright colors with white. Photo, courtesy Sally Pleet.

Right: "Twelve Tribes of Israel," an appliquéd tapestry hanging made by a group of women from Congregation Keneseth in Allentown, Pennsylvania. Patterns were traced from carvings on sanctuary doors. Fabrics used include fake fur, heavy upholstery velvets, brocades, gold cloth, Lurex, and knitted fabrics; parts of the designs were padded, and a great deal of embroidery was added for enrichment and details. Blocks were joined in strips and mounted on heavy monk's cloth; all seams are covered by heavy twisted cord. Photo, courtesy of Helen Pell and Hess Brothers.

Below: Finishing touches for banners. Add trinkets, bells, tassels, pom-poms, beads, or ornaments to bottom edges for a novel, eye-catching design.

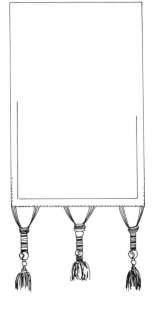

Left: "They Danced, Then Dropped" by Dawn Beecher. The legs of the dancers hang down freely from the bottom of the banner. To the far right is an old skull and crossbones complete with skeleton body, waiting. Photo, Susie Montgomery.

Below left: A landscape picture, "Bay with Mountains," appliquéd by Madge Huntington. In misty blues, grays, lavender, and greens. Size, 76 by 114.5 cm (30 by 45 in.). Photo, courtesy Madge Huntington.

Below: "Sea Life." Shapes of various sea creatures are appliquéd with bright colors on black ground, then surrounded by two borders, the inner one red, the outer one black. By Sara Cibelli for Patience Corner Patchwork. Photo, Sara Cibelli.

announce or celebrate an important event, proclaim a basic tenet or belief, or express your love for someone.

12. To make a casing for an unlined banner or hanging, finish or hem the sides first. Now, fold over the top to the wrong side; the size of the casing or hem is determined by the size of the rod or dowel you use. Measure, then pin, then stitch from side to side and slip the rod through the opening.

13. If your banner or hanging needs a little extra weight to hang properly, you can also make a casing across the bottom and slip a rod through; usually these bottom dowels do not extend

House portrait by Carole Pugliese. A New Orleans French Quarter house of cottons in pale blue, bright red, with lace doilies, edgings, and insertions, appliquéd on a gray cotton ground. Photo, Carole Pugliese.

Steps in mitering corners on a hemmed finish for a wall hanging. **a.** Overcast raw edges, turn hem to right side, and press along hem fold lines on sides and bottom. **b.** Open folded end out so that edges meet, press diagonally (dotted line), then stitch, keeping hem free from rest of fabric. **c.** Trim excess fabric from corner seam, press open, then turn hem to wrong side. **d.** Mitered hem ready for final stitching.

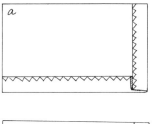
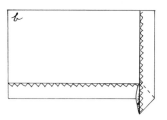

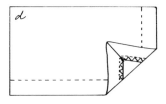

through the openings, but are enclosed in the casing, like the bottom of window shades. For either a top or bottom casing, or both, be sure to plan ahead and leave extra material—at least 10 to 12.5 cm (4 to 5 in.) for each one. If you forget to do this and still want casings, face the banner ends with strips of material.

14. Appliqué hangings can also be mounted or stretched. Again, always allow extra material around the sides. You can buy stretcher bars at art supply shops; they come in many sizes. Lay your appliqué face down on a flat, smooth surface; center the joined stretcher bars over it. Bring edges of appliqué up over bars. Use tacks or staples, and start with a tack in the center of each side before you begin to work your way to the corners.

You can also use plywood, hardboard, or Masonite. Cut it to size. Put your appliqué face down, as described previously. Center the board on the wrong side; there should be a margin of 2.5 to 5 cm (1 to 2 in.) of fabric. With a small brush paint around the edges of the Masonite or plywood with white glue. Pull fabric edges down smoothly over this, working from the center out on each side. Trim bulk from corners. Let it dry thoroughly before handling.

15

SMALLER TREASURES, ENDLESS PLEASURES...

PILLOWS

Most pillows are friendly and cuddly; they are warm invitations and offbeat, unusual accents in a home. They can be used in any room of a house or apartment, in cars, boats, trains, or planes. They come in all sizes and shapes, plain or fancy, and in any and all fabrics. They can be works of art or purely utilitarian. Pillows can have the shape of human or animal figures, or the shape of fruits, vegetables, or flowers. They can also be shaped geometrically—square, rectangular, triangular, or round. With such great variety in style and pattern available, they can be a lot of fun to make; they are also dandy gifts.

You can use almost any fabric for a pillow; what materials go into it probably will depend on where the pillow is to be used. Many combinations are possible. You can appliqué the front of the pillow and leave the back plain; you can appliqué both sides so it won't matter which shows. You can appliqué and add quilting to the front or to both. It's up to you. Here are some instructions for a basic pillow.

Basic Pillow. For easy sewing, the front and back must be the same size. Work on a flat surface. Place the two sections right sides together, match up the corners, and pin in place. If you plan to stuff the pillow with polyfil or kapok, stitch the two sides together all around the edge but leave an opening on one side large enough to get your hand through. This is for stuffing. Close the opening later with slip stitches.

If you prefer to use a separate pillow form for the inside, leave one entire side open.

You can add boxing to a basic pillow shape. This is a strip usually from 5 to 10 cm (2 to 4 in.) wide sewed between the front and back of a pillow. The strip must, of course, be long enough to go around the pillow, plus two seam allowances. For instance, if your pillow is 30.5 cm (12 in.) square, you need four times this measurement, plus 2.5 cm (1 in.) for the two seam allowances. Sew the ends of the strip together and plan to have the seam fall in the middle of one side, not at a corner. Now, measure and notch the corner placements on both long edges of the boxing; the notches will ensure even placement of pillow top and bottom. Stitch one side of the boxing all the way around the pillow top, right sides together. Match the boxing to the pillow back, then

Appliquéd pillow from India. White section is cut "snowflake," folded-paper style, appliquéd without seam on black ground. Fish in center is bright yellow. Collection of the author. Photo, Stubby Crowe.

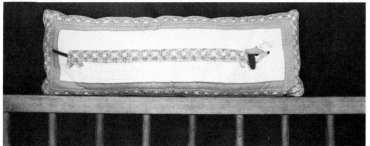

"Long Dog" pillow. Designed and made by the author. Dog of olive green calico, hand appliquéd to light blue cotton ground. Outlined with solid red and calico border; hand quilted. Photo, Stubby Crowe.

"Arrow Collar Man" pillow by Margaret Cusack. Cottons, velvets, and satins, machine appliquéd to black ground. Photo, courtesy Margaret Cusack.

Right: Wedding pillow, on the left, red appliqué on natural muslin ground. "People" pillow, on the right, hand appliquéd and quilted. White, red, yellow, and black people touch hands in a circle on a gray background. Both by the author. Photo, Mary Alice Fisher.

Above: Ruffling basted to appliquéd pillow top. Raw edges of ruffling are lined up with raw edges of pillow and basted all around. Backing is placed over this, with edges and corners matched. Leave bottom side open to accommodate a commercial pillow form, or leave smaller opening along fourth side for stuffing with polyfil. When pillow cover is turned right side out, ruffle will be along edge. Same procedure can be used for piping or welting.

Below: "Humpty Dumpty" pillow designed and made by Jody Schnautz. Hand appliquéd in cottons and blends. Photo, Mary Alice Fisher.

stitch around three sides, or three and part of the fourth, and stuff as you would a basic pillow.

You can also add piping, welting, a ruffle, or fringe to a basic pillow or a boxed pillow. Suppose you want to add a ruffle to a basic pillow. Place the ruffling against the pillow front, with right sides touching, and the unfinished edge of the ruffle lined up with the raw edge of the pillow. Machine-baste this in place. Now put the pillow back over this, so that the right side of the back is against the right side of the front; the ruffling will be between the two layers. Pin in place. Turn the pillow over and stitch the back to the front from the front side; the machine basting will be the guide for you to follow.

You can use a zipper or a length of snap tape to close the pillowcase if you prefer; stitch either to one edge each of the pillow front and back before you joint them; flat surfaces are easier, particularly for zipper application. When the zipper is in, joint the front and back of the pillow, but remember to open the zipper so that you can turn the pillow.

Poly- or fiberfil is an easy and inexpensive stuffing for a pillow; also, since it is washable, you don't have to take the pillow apart when it's ready for the laundry. A word or two about the stuffing, however: stuff by the handful, and start in the corners, then work your way around the edges. Keep on stuffing long after you think you have enough, for the polyfil has a tendency to settle. Also, if you don't want to risk a lumpy look, use a layer of quilt batting to make an extra pillowcase. Cut the batting strip 2.5 cm (1 in.) wider than the pillow, and twice as long; fold the strip horizontally, then, *by hand*, catch the sides together. Leave the bottom edge open. Insert this batting case in your pillow envelope, then add the polyfil stuffing. Slip-stitch the opening closed.

BAGS

Bags—the carryall to carry all! I have an affinity for them, all colors, shapes, and sizes; I never have too many. Years ago there seemed to be a difference between a purse-bag and a tote or shopping bag, but no more. They are practically interchangeable. If there is a difference now, it might be that a purse is a little smaller, but I wouldn't count on it.

Bags, like pillows, come in all fabrics, all shapes. You can carry them in your hand, over your arm, over your shoulder, or on your back. Most of them will tote anything from books to groceries; others are designed specifically for certain contents—sewing or needlework, overnight supplies, swim and beach wear, sports, picnics—you name it, there's a bag for it. You make a basic bag almost like you'd make a basic pillow, except that you add handles and you leave one side (the top) open. You *can* close it, of course, by adding a zipper, a drawstring, a loop and button, or a flap. Your bag also can be appliquéd by either hand or machine, or it can be appliquéd and quilted. You can add a lining if you like, and you can add pockets—to the inside, the outside, or the ends. You can also add boxing between the two sides to increase carrying space.

The ubiquitous, standard paper shopping bag makes an excellent pattern, but if you don't want to bother taking one apart, the following instructions will tell you how to make a simple, basic bag with a lining and two handles for carrying by hand.

Cut two fabric rectangles twice the length of the bag; one rectangle is bag fabric, the other is lining. If you want a pocket on the lining, stitch it on now while you have a flat piece of fabric. Make the fabric handles—cut two rectangles of bag fabric 38 cm (15 in.) long and 7.5 cm (3 in.) wide. This allows for seams. Fold each rectangle lengthwise with right side inside, then machine-stitch the long side 1.3 cm (½ in.) from the raw edge. Do not stitch across the ends. Now turn these tubes right side out and press, keeping the seam along one edge. Now mark the middle point on each end of the bag rectangle. This is for handle placement. Measure 6.5 cm (2½ in.) on each side of the middle point, and pin the handle ends to these, one on each side. Machine-stitch across the ends 1.3 cm (½ in.) in from raw edge, for security. Now put the bag rectangle on a flat surface, with appliqué or outside on top. Lay the lining rectangle against this, right sides facing; the handles will be between the two fabric layers. Now stitch around the rectangle, leaving an opening on one long side for turning. After stitching, trim seams closely, and cut excess fabric across corners. Turn rectangle to right side, and press. Slip-stitch the opening closed. Now fold the rectangle horizontally with the right side inside, and, by machine, stitch the two sides closed. You'll be stitching with lining outside; when through, turn bag and *voilà!* The finished tote!

This is a fast and easy way to make a lined tote in one

Above: **Folding camp stool covered with bright yellow canvas, by the author. The butterfly is cut from medium-weight printed cotton and appliquéd with machine zigzag stitch. The butterfly's feelers are also machine stitched. Photo, Stubby Crowe.**
Below: **Needlework or general carry-all bag by the author. Bag foundation is red vinyl with zipper. Front foundation is canvas designed for needlepoint; a section of an old Victorian crazy block was used instead. Photo, Stubby Crowe.**

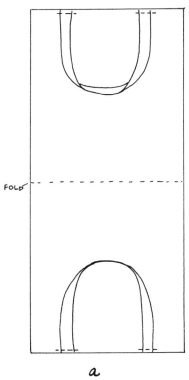

a

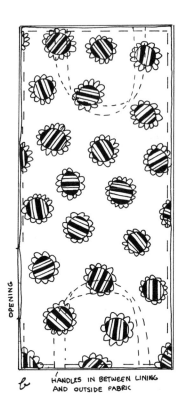

b HANDLES IN BETWEEN LINING AND OUTSIDE FABRIC

c

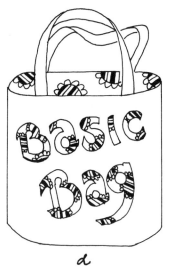

d

Basic bag construction. **a.** Rectangle long enough for front and back of bag. Finished handles stitched in place. **b.** Lining fabric placed against outside of bag, right sides together. Handles are between lining and outside fabric.

Rectangle is stitched all the way around except for a side opening for turning. Seams are trimmed closely, then bag turned and pressed. Opening closed by hand. **c.** Right sides together, bag is folded horizontally and sides stitched. Note stitching (dotted lines) across bottom corners to round off. **d.** Finished bag turned to right side, ready to use.

operation. If you prefer a shoulder bag to a hand one, simply lengthen the handles or straps.

If you want to add boxing to the bag, sew the boxing in place on each long side of the rectangle, and add the lining later. Mark the bag rectangle to correspond with the bottom end and width of the boxing, and clip each bottom corner of the boxing almost to the stitching or seam line. This will help you stitch around the corners as you come to them.

If you want to expand your bag wardrobe, you can coordinate by adding a duffel, garment, and shoe bag, or anything else that strikes your fancy.

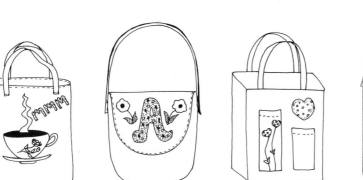

a. Simple bag with handles. **b.** Bag with flap to cover opening. **c.** Bag with boxing joining front and back and outside pockets. **d.** Boxed bag with zipper outside pocket, one end strap for hand or shoulder carrying.

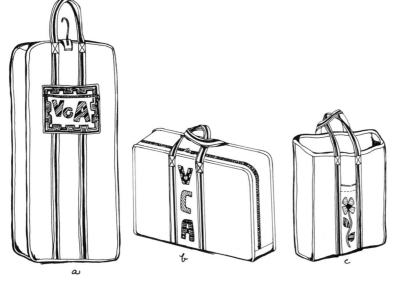

a. Garment bag. **b.** Overnight or weekend bag. **c.** Tote to match.

a. Bag with shoulder straps cut in one with front and back, ends finished off and tied. **b.** Picnic bag. Could be lined with vinyl.

Panda bag for lucky child with a honey of an outside pocket.

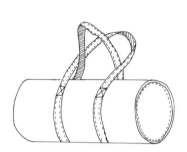

Right: Round duffel bag.

Far right: Shoulder bag by the author. Machine appliquéd with bright cutouts from printed fabric, sewed to rose pink cotton. Inside section is closed by zipper. Photo, Stubby Crowe.

Left: Cat Bag, by Barbara Hester. Two cats, one red and the other yellow and white, sprawl comfortably on a green background. There are two borders, a yellow print with blue corners and a red print. Machine appliquéd. The bag has wooden handles. Size, 40 by 35 cm (15 by 13 in.). Photo, courtesy Barbara Hester.
Right: An unusual tote bag, designed by Laurice Keyloun. Bag of jade green Ultrasuede fabric, with mola panel appliquéd to front. Photo, Stubby Crowe.

BOXES

Sometimes it's nice to "think small"; fabric boxes are fun to make, and they, like pillows and bags, are also charming and unusual little gifts. Square or rectangular boxes are easier to make; if you must have a round one, cover a ready-made box rather than start from scratch.

The basic box. Let's try one 15- or 18-cm (6- or 7-in.) square. First, you have to have something sturdy for the sides or your box won't be able to stand alone. Photo-mat board works very well. Your local framing shop may have a lot of odds and ends and scraps that would be suitable for box making; ask them to cut the scraps to size for you. You need six squares, four sides and a top and bottom.

You also need two pieces of fabric for each square; one will be on the outside of the box, the other will be the lining. Cut the squares 13 mm (½ in.) larger all the way around to allow for seams. Appliqué your designs on the outside fabric pieces before they are joined; you do not need appliqué on the bottom.

Now, join together two squares of fabric for each cardboard or photo-mat board; place the lining square against the right side of the appliquéd square, and stitch around three sides, leaving the

"Glenora's Box," hexagon-shaped box of felt, with felt appliquéd design and lettering. Side panels are lightly stuffed with polyfil; sides are joined together with buttonhole stitch. By the author. Felt by Continental. Photo, Stubby Crowe.

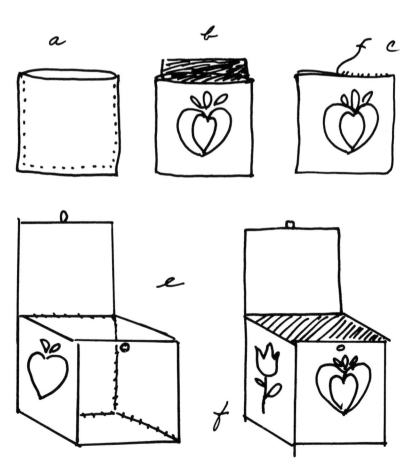

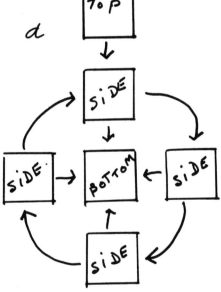

Basic box. **a.** Six fabric squares of equal size, five of them appliquéd; six lining squares. Appliquéd square and lining square stitched, right sides together, around three sides; turned, pressed. **b.** Photo mat board inserted in envelope, and polyfil stuffing added on both sides of cardboard for soft, rounded effect. **c.** Opening stitched by hand. **d.** Joining of squares to make a box. **e.** How seams appear. **f.** Finished box.

Above: Four blocks by the author. The block on the right is a crazy patch with fabrics placed at random around the center block of an apple print. Embroidery stitches of herringbone and feather, worked in mercerized sewing thread, cover the joins. The bottom block is spiderweb; the four kite-shaped patches in each triangle make the completed center design when the triangles are sewed together. Foundation blocks were unbleached muslin. Photo, Stubby Crowe.

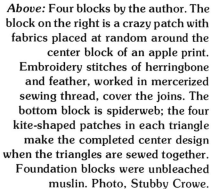

"Christmas Cards" by the author. A set of small appliquéd pictures, each 17 by 19 cm (6½ by 7½ in.), in a variety of fabrics from felt and cotton to silk. Embroidery stitches bring out details. All hand sewn in appliqué and reverse appliqué. Photos, Stubby Crowe.

bottom edge open. This makes a little pillowcase or envelope. Turn to the right side, insert the photo-mat board, then stuff lightly with polyfil or scraps of batting—just enough to give it a smooth, rounded appearance. Slip-stitch the opening closed. Do not put any stuffing in the lining side of the top or the box may not close properly.

With a strong, close whipping stitch, join the bottom edge of each of the four sides to the sides of the bottom of the box. Now fold up the sides until they meet, and join them together the same

Other "smaller treasures" for appliqué—a chair, a window shade.

way. If you want decorative stitching, use a herringbone, feather, or Cretan embroidery stitch to hold the sides together; keep the stitches small to create a lacing effect, and use perle cotton or crochet thread. A small curved needle may help here, too, instead of the customary straight ones. When the four sides are joined together, attach the top only along its bottom edge; otherwise it won't open and close properly. Sew on a tiny braid frog or a loop and button for closing.

"Glenora's Box" (see page 135) has a hexagon top and bottom, but six straight rectangular sides, so that the construction was simple.

If you use felt or Ultrasuede for a box, cut the pieces exactly to photo-mat size; you do not need seam allowances. You could also add a zipper to a fabric box in much the same way you add one to a pillow or bag; plan ahead, however, so that you can sew the zipper in place before the box is sewed together.

16

SOLOMON IN ALL HIS GLORY...!

Appliqué on Clothing

We've often heard, "We are what we eat," or "We are what we do." These statements undoubtedly have a ring of truth, but no less important is "We are what we wear." Clothes not only are a practical necessity, but they identify us—and have for centuries. There are the elegant, luxurious "uniforms" of royalty, the Church, the theater, and the arts. There is a type of uniform worn by working middle classes, another type by peasants and farmers. Such "uniforms" are identified by fabrics, style or design, workmanship and detail—the same standards we set for other kinds of artistic needlework. It's natural for most of us to want to upgrade ourselves, and if we can't afford certain types of clothes, we can copy or get ideas from them and adapt them to suit our own needs. All of this combines into what we call "fashion"—a fickle though delightful mistress. We defy hard times with bright colors and carefree styles; we deliberately reject accepted standards of the times and go our own way. Men and women both have long used needle and thread to express themselves in one form or another. You don't *have* to confine the work of your hand to the wall or the bed; you can wear your art.

Several years ago the young people in our country brought about a fashion revolution when they adopted blue jeans as a uniform. A wave of jeans swept over the country; denim was the great leveler. Jeans questioned authority and tradition, expressed rebellion, and also provided comfort, security, and anonymity. You couldn't tell the rich from the poor, the smart from the dumb, and, often, the boys from the girls. Everybody looked alike—but not for long. Denims gradually took on the marks of the wearers—they were studded, embroidered, patched, appliquéd, and beaded, and finally the Levi contest established once and for all the validity of art and decoration for clothing.

Museums throughout the country maintain permanent collections of period costumes and styles; new exhibits are constantly being mounted and shown to an eager public—not only American styles, but many from other countries. One of the outstanding recent exhibits was that of the Russian costumes shown at the Metropolitan Museum in New York; it was breathtaking to see the exquisite and imaginative appliqué, embroidery, and beading that was lavished on most of the garments.

The happy thing about this is that you can do as little or as

much as you like on your own clothes. You can add something to a purchased article if you can't or don't want to make your own; as in all kinds of needlework discussed in this book, it's up to you. You can put your own stamp on your clothes with an appliquéd design on a pocket, belt, or collar. Even small children take great pleasure in little designs on their clothes—a flower, a balloon, or a lollipop. They may know little about color and form, but they learn at a tender age to enjoy it.

You may be somewhat limited in appliquéing a purchased garment—it depends actually on what it is and how it's made. An unlined jacket is easy enough to handle because it opens up and you can get to it. Skirts are not difficult either, and shirts and blouses offer all kinds of possibilities. Pants and slacks can be a problem simply because of the way they are made, but it is easier to appliqué by hand than by machine when tackling something like this—especially the leg sections.

Even if you are not an experienced sewer, many garments can be easily made just by straight seaming. A dirndl skirt is a good example. You need a rectangle for the skirt body—the length of the fabric should be roughly twice your waist measurement or less. This gives you ample fabric to gather or pleat into a waistband. The two ends of the rectangle are sewed together to make the back seam, usually with a zipper inserted at the top. The width of this fabric length actually becomes the skirt length for you; decide how long you want the skirt and cut accordingly, adding a little extra for a hem. Before the back seaming or gathering is done, while the fabric is still a flat rectangle, plan your appliqué design and sew it down, much as you would if working on a banner or hanging.

If your skirt is shaped (A-line or flared) and has two pieces instead of one (separate front and back), then sew the right side seam together and work your design as before. When you've finished the appliqué, seam the left side and finish the skirt. The fan skirt (Plate 11) was made this way. It is of wool double-knit fabric. The right side seam was stitched and pressed, then the skirt was spread out on a table. The appliqués are five fans, adapted

Children's clothes appliquéd with charming and simple designs to give a personal touch.

Robe, designed and made by the author, inspired by Lady Sagami's verse:
"Whose sleeves do you enfold
While leaving me to lie here night after night
Alone on my widest robe?"
Robe of black wool challis; sleeves are strips of white, rose pink, and gray challis stitched together, with large floral appliqué of same wool. Sleeves are lined with white china silk; the obi is pink, dark red, and gray, wrapped and tied. Photo, Stubby Crowe.

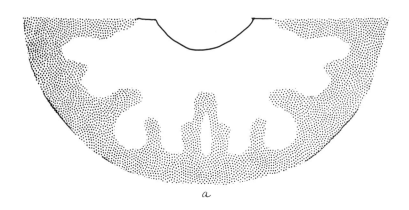

Right: **a.** Half-circle skirt with Hawaiian-type appliqué border. **b.** Same half-circle skirt with appliquéd band inserted.

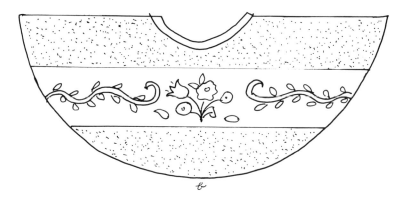

Below, center: A wool poncho suit by the author. Of black-and-white Donegal tweed, appliquéd with cotton prints in shades of red, and black and white. Abstract shapes were cut freely and several sections were stuffed and machine quilted. All raw edges were covered with bias binding made of a rose cotton print fabric. Poncho is unlined. Photo, Stubby Crowe.

Below, far right: Purchased navy work shirt, with appliqués in various fabrics added by the author. Machine zigzag and decorative stitches used. Photo, Stubby Crowe.

Below: Heavy white cotton skirt by Ardis James. Circular patches of various black-and-white printed fabrics were cut freely, pinned in place, and machine appliquéd. Border is solid black. Photo, Stubby Crowe.

from that timeless quilt pattern. The pattern was enlarged and all the pieces appliquéd to a lightweight ground fabric—none of which shows. I used satins, velveteens, wools, and silks; hand embroidery covers the joins of the fan spokes, and the "handles" are decorated with machine embroidery stitches. The fans were then fitted in place on the bottom of the skirt and the skirt fabric trimmed to conform with the lines of the appliquéd sections.

Evening jacket designed and made by the author. Crazy patch appliqué technique, with velvets, silks, and brocades; patches are further decorated with hand-embroidery stitches and some sequins and beads to emphasize fabric design. Photo, Stubby Crowe.

Woman's vest, hat, and man's formal dinner jacket made by the Cuna Indian women for Laurice Keyloun. True mola techniques with designs appliquéd with several layers of cotton fabrics. Photos, Stubby Crowe.

Bottom right: Hand-quilted cotton vest with appliquéd border patches, by the author. Photo, Stubby Crowe.

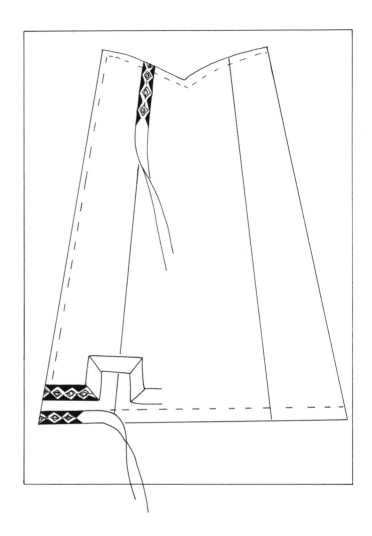

Right and below right: Trim applied over seams while skirt sections are flat.

Below: Skirt and vest trimmed with appliquéd bands, or braid or ribbon.

stitch braid on an angle, right sides together, to make mitered corners.

stitching direction for left hand corner

stitching direction for right hand corner

turn to right side + stitch in place on pattern.

Far left: Lined vest; felt appliqué on wool would be a handsome combination.

Left: Appliquéd bands or borders sewed to shawl collar, bottom of sleeves, and jacket hem.

Below: Hawaiian-type appliqué on evening dress. Same type of design could be sewed with reverse appliqué technique; design could also be adapted to shorter version of dress.

These were machine-stitched in place along the top, with bias binding covering the raw edges. After the left side seam was sewed, I bound the bottom edge in black wool braid.

I adapted a quilt design again for a cotton skirt with an appliquéd border. The skirt is dirndl style, and the final width was determined by the fit of the appliqué sections rather than hip measurements. Hexagons were cut from various fabrics, then appliquéd with simple designs, by hand. When the blocks were joined, they were pinned in place along the bottom edge of the skirt, with a layer of quilt batting between the skirt and the hexagons. The strip was then hand quilted, and again, bias tape covered the raw edges at the top and was machine top-stitched in place. This quilted border is lined, and the lining also serves to finish the bottom edge. A fabric rectangle, long enough and wide enough to cover the appliquéd strip, was placed right side down against the right side of the appliqués and pinned in place. The bottom edge then was seamed by machine, following the zigzag edge of the long hexagons. Afterward, I trimmed the seams closely, then stitched the back seam of the skirt, keeping the lining free. The lining folds up inside the skirt, hiding all those knots and stitches, and is caught by hand to the top edge of the appliqué.

Now, let yourself go with some decorations on your own clothes; whether they are off the rack or off the bolt, they'll be unmistakably yours!

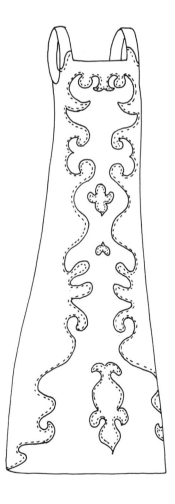

17

THE LITTLEST ANGELS:

Children and Appliqué

We see our children as a link to our own immortality, and indeed they are; through them, we persist in the life stream. We often indulge them; they are the hope, the world of the future. We strive for good schools; and we encourage the sports, the music, the dancing classes and dramas, and the art classes. Children, from babyhood, are bubbling over with creative energy, and we try to channel it in many ways. I've always loved children's art; they have a most direct and refreshing way of drawing, uncluttered by perspective or balance. They get right to the point, and often their drawings bear messages many of us overlook or don't understand.

From the time they are old enough to hold a pencil or crayon, we encourage them to draw, to put on paper what they think or see. This continues from kindergarten throughout the school years in various media—crayons, pastels, watercolors, oils, silk screen; seldom has it occurred to teachers or others in the school system to give children a needle and thread instead of a brush or crayon. Only in the past few years have appliqué and simple embroidery been introduced, but at last it is catching on—more and more schools are using it as an art form or recreation or for refining hand skills, and the children love it. They experience textures in needlework, something they don't get with paint and paper. Handling and working with different fabrics, yarns, and threads add dimension to their creativity. Colors are "ready-made" for them, too; they don't have to be mixed, and this, especially at the beginning, helps a child to develop color sense.

The impetus in developing and establishing such needlecraft as part of the school curriculum was due in part to the American Bicentennial celebrations—the same celebrations that fostered the return of the pictorial quilt—but one enterprising woman, Jean Linden, a librarian in an urban ghetto school of New York City, went a step further. She saw in needlework an exciting way to expand a child's interest in reading and learning. A quilter herself, she chose fifth-graders for a quilt-making venture. Each child was allowed to choose a favorite story or storybook character as subject matter for appliqué. The librarian helped them draw or trace the designs from library books to be used as patterns: Ms. Linden gave each child a cotton square for background, felt scraps for appliqué, and needles and yarn. In little more than a week's time, Ms. Linden had forty quilt blocks ready to assemble.

She pushed together four large tables in the library so that the children could spread the blocks out and arrange them; she showed them how to join the blocks to make the quilt, and while they worked, she told them stories of colonial times.

This Story Quilt (see below) set off a chain reaction. Parents and teachers alike wanted to make quilts; meanwhile, Ms. Linden was invited to demonstrate her learning and teaching methods at an educational conference in New York. She chose five girls to demonstrate quilting and dressed them in colonial costume; all this, in turn, led to a television appearance on an educational channel. Since then, successive fifth-graders of this school have turned out a number of quilts; elementary schools all over the country have begun to explore the learning possibilities of needlework and simple appliqué for children.

The lessons don't stop with history and English. Children, working together on any group project, must cooperate, or nothing gets done. In a physical sense, they learn to work closely with other children; on another level, they must recognize the importance of other children and their work. Less talented children are stimulated and encouraged; this group participation and exchange have an important influence in helping a child to mature. Early on, a child learns pride in accomplishment. Whenever he expresses himself on any artistic or creative level, he is in effect saying, "Look at me! I did this. I count, I'm somebody."

The drawings or colorings children do at school or at home are a delightful and endless source of ideas and design: translating these pictures into fabric delights any child and adds to his or her self-confidence. Keep your child's drawings where you can study them and decide how best to use them. A single picture can become a pillow top, a framed hanging, or a block in a quilt or banner. Lay a piece of tracing paper over the drawing, and trace it. Use the original as a color guide, and cut the tracing apart to use

The Peter Quilt, made by children in P.S. 48 Queens Elementary School with help and direction from Jean Linden, the librarian. Concept from the "Peter" stories by Ezra Jack Keats; the blocks illustrate incidents in the book. Figures are of felt appliquéd on cotton. Photo, Kim Blanchard.

Story Quilt made by fifth grade of P.S. 48 Queens Elementary School under the supervision of Jean Linden. Each block depicts a character or scene from a favorite story. Felt appliqués on cotton ground. Photo, Kim Blanchard.

as a pattern. Details too small for appliqué work can be easily handled with simple embroidery.

Of course you don't need to confine yourself to your child's work for designs. You can make a charming and simple quilt, hanging, or banner for your child's room and incorporate favorite toys or books or activities into it. A very small child would love a soft fabric book, the pages appliquéd with ABC's, numbers, or symbols of the holidays—a Santa Claus, a jack-o'-lantern, a birthday candle. You can make wonderful masks and costumes with appliqué; simple appliquéd dolls, toys, and puppets can add a great deal to a child's pleasure. "Soft" game boards—for

a. Basic doll shape. Two pieces of fabric cut for front and back; face, hair, and clothes appliquéd and embroidered before doll is seamed or stuffed. **b.** Basic doll with legs added. Legs made separately, shoes appliquéd, legs stuffed, then inserted in openings at bottom of dress. **c.** Arms made and stuffed separately, then added. **d.** Same doll, yarn hair and jewelry added.

Parcheesi or checkers—can be packed for picnics or vacations. Play rugs, appliquéd with village or landscape backgrounds, offer endless hours of entertainment with the addition of toy trains and boats, farm animals, and the like. Storage is simple; when your little one gets bored, the rug can be hung on the wall or rolled up and stored on a closet shelf.

There are a lot of possibilities in game banners for the small fry; children love the blindfold games, and most of us remember

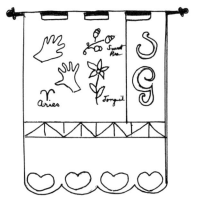

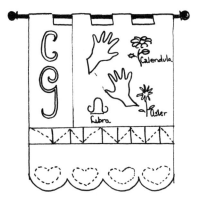

Above: **Banners for Sara and Celia. Their own hands are used for design elements; also their initials, zodiac signs, and flowers of their birth months.**

Top left: **A drawing of "Clifford's Castle" by seven-year-old Brett Foster.** *Left:* **The quilted appliqué block his mother, Mary Helen Foster, made from the drawing. Both photos, Mary Helen Foster.**

Alphabet counterpane, by Janie Burke.
A mixture of satins, velvets, silks, and
antique lace; embellished with buttons,
bells, and French knots. Photo,
Michael James, courtesy Janie Burke.

pinning the tail on the donkey at neighborhood or school parties.
A fabric version of this would make a charming wall decoration
and still be handy to have around when children are playing
together. You don't have to stay with donkeys; any animal will do.
Cut a simple shape from felt or scraps of woven fabric, and stitch it
to a background material. Make tails from felt, and to keep track
of them, stitch a pocket on one corner of the game banner for
storage.

Another type of game for children is similar to the play rug idea.
Try a simple landscape—for instance, the top of a fabric rectangle
would be the sky, with the sun's position marked or embroidered.
A tree can grow along one side, with a long horizontal branch; put
a bird's nest on the branch. On the bottom third of the background rectangle, use a shade of blue felt or cotton fabric for
water, and show the outlines of two or three fish. Now, make
small bean-bag shapes of bird's eggs, fish, and the sun. These are
easily made from two layers of felt. Whip-stitch the edges
together, or stitch around the edge by machine; leave a small
opening and fill the shape with beans, pebbles, or rice, then sew
the opening closed. When children play the game, the rug or
banner is on the floor. Blindfold each child in turn; each tosses the
little bean bags one by one and, of course, tries to get the eggs in
the nest, the sun in the sky, and the fish in the water.

Children also love appliquéd designs on their clothes. If you sew for your children, it is easy to put a simple design on fabric after the garment is cut out—or even before, if the area is small—a bird, a flower, a balloon, an ice cream cone, or a kite. Any such simple shapes could be added easily to ready-made dresses or overalls.

All kinds of masks and costumes are possible with imaginative use of appliqué. Draw the mask design on paper first so that you'll be reasonably sure of a proper fit; children have small faces, and it's important not only that the mask fit their features well but that they will be able to see when wearing it. If you use lightweight fabric, mount it over cardboard to give it some body. A better choice of material is heavyweight Pellon or, once again, felt. These masks can be tied around a child's head (even "grownup" children love to wear them) or attached at the top to a "beanie" or skull-cap type of head covering. Add an elaborate headdress or hat over such a foundation, and the whole thing is easy enough to manage.

Simple costumes are easy to make from sheets or a double length of fabric. Such outfits have only a front and back; they slip over the head and possibly are ankle-length—not long enough to trip over. Measure your child from top of head to ankles, and measure the length of his arms, then cut out the costume using the drawing as a guide. Appliqué a face on an oval of Pellon or felt, and stitch it to the front of the costume before you join the front and back together. Such a simple outfit can be adapted to almost any occasion by varying the color and fabric of the basic garment

"Mother Goose Rhymes" by Martha Opdahl. Hand-appliquéd, hand-quilted wall hanging. Each of the six blocks depicts a nursery rhyme and is appliquéd to light background, stripped and bordered in bright yellow.

a, b. Two fabric masks to tie in place.
c. Fabric mask to slip over the head.

Above: "David's Fantasy Farm" quilt designed and made by Barbara Hester; an award winner in the Warren, Michigan, 1976 show. Hand appliquéd and quilted; assorted cottons and cotton blends. David is in the center surrounded by his fantasies and held in with a bright red border. Size, approximately 160 by 240 cm (65 by 85 in.). Photo, courtesy Barbara Hester.

Above right: "Family of Dolls" crib quilt by Sybil Sermos. The center panel is light blue, with an appliquéd house, tree, shrubbery, and a flag flying from the porch. A walk leads to the water's edge where a little sailboat bounces along through whitecaps. On either side of the center panel is a parade of dolls, both "human" and animal, a charming panorama for any child. Hand appliquéd and quilted. Photo, courtesy Sybil Sermos.

Right: Math Quilt made by fifth-graders in P.S. 48 Queens Elementary School. Each block is appliquéd with a mathematical symbol, shape, or number. Planned and coordinated by Jean Linden. Photo, Kim Blanchard.

and the character of the face. Try an animal face made of felt and use fake fur for the costume—in other words, use your imagination.

All children love the thrill of camping or sleeping outdoors; even if they don't sleep overnight, they like to set up temporary camp or housekeeping in their own little hideaways. Stitch an appliqué on your child's pup tent, or make an indoor playhouse by covering a card table. You need five squares of fabric for this—one for the top of the table, one for each side to fit from tabletop to floor. Cut an opening in one side for a door, and add as much or as little as you like to the rest of the fabric house.

Most children have "security blankets"—not necessarily real blankets, but cuddly dolls, stuffed toys, pillows, or little nap pads they cherish. Such belongings assume far greater importance than their intrinsic worth. They are real friends to a child, something familiar in an unfamiliar world; they are dependable. Many children, long after they are grown, cherish these "security blankets" for the sentimental and nostalgic memories they evoke: something handmade by Mother gets an extra dose of devotion and care, for it is a symbol of love.

Doll quilt by Carter Houck. A miniature Rose-of-Sharon pattern suggested by a collection of quilt blocks in the Museum of the Big Bend in Alpine, Texas, worked by Mrs. A. G. Smith. Quilt measures 38 by 63.5 cm (15 by 25 in.). Four hearts are quilted around the rose. All handmade for the author's doll bed, which she received when she was five years old. Photo, Stubby Crowe.

18

DECISIONS, DECISIONS!

To Keep, Give Away, or Sell?

Well, friend, by this time you've been through a lot, reading and learning about appliqué, and, I hope, experimenting with it as you went along. Experimenting isn't always easy or comfortable, but it's exciting—and sometimes tiring. I hope ideas are beginning to come to you faster than you can handle them—if this is the case, don't let them get away. Jot them down, and they'll be waiting.

If you're really hooked on appliqué, your house or apartment is probably full of it; effective and attractive as it is, there *is* a limit—but not without other possibilities. If you have all the pillows, banners, and quilts you need at the moment, and you want to keep on making things, then consider marketing your work. The photographs in this book have already exposed you to the work of many talented artists and craftsmen; it's comforting to remember they all started at the beginning, too. Don't moan and groan if you don't think you have enough talent to go commercial with your work—it isn't *all* talent; a great deal of what any of us accomplish comes from self-discipline, just buckling down to the job and getting it done.

You probably have decided by now what you like to do best; some people want to make quilts to sell, others are staggered at the thought of such large projects. Perhaps there is one special technique that appeals to you—reverse appliqué or Hawaiian appliqué—you're the one to decide that. When you've chosen an area of appliqué, it's time to think of your market.

Who would buy your product? How much would someone pay for it? Where could others find it? Where could they find you? Before there is a demand for your work, people have to see and appreciate it. Go to your local library or bank and see if either is interested in an exhibit—most will be. Enter a juried craft exhibit or show. Most juried shows are pretty good, for a committee has to examine and pass on your work before they give you permission to enter. If in the beginning you are rejected, find out why, and raise your standards so that it won't happen again. Sometimes craftsmen are turned down, not because of inferior work, but because the things they make don't fit in a certain category. Check on this before you submit your entries.

Many times a craft show committee will consider only slide entries, so if you want to expand into a part-time business and make a little mad money on the side, be businesslike in your approach. Learn to use a camera—there are special techniques for craft photography, and you should get some instruction as you practice. If you can't or won't master a camera along with everything else, get a friend to do it for you. When you've finished something you're proud of, take several identical slides. You'll want one for your records, and you'll have two or three extra to submit later on. Original slides are always better than duplicates, and this is easier to do than to take one slide only, then trot down to the store to have it copied.

Finish your work properly and professionally, whether it's mounted, bound, or framed. Keep track of the time it took to make, and decide how much money your time is worth. I hate to say this, but you'll probably never get paid the full amount; few people could afford it. You'll have to come to terms with this, but remember that if you are working at home, you don't have to pay the overhead necessary in a shop or studio.

If you overprice, your work won't sell, so try to be realistic—and then stick with it. Often a customer won't buy the first time around but may very well come back. If you are exhibiting locally, potential customers will see your work; be prepared with a price in case you are approached.

Craft fairs are good testing grounds, but, as I suggested, try for a juried one. Most craft shows charge an entry fee or a percentage of sales; find out about this. You should have some props, too, depending on what you're selling—or trying to sell. Have a table or two, or a place to hang things; make your booth or area as attractive and eye-catching as possible. Have plenty of business cards handy—a card may lead a customer back to you some day.

More and more people—and not always young ones—are beginning to establish themselves as professional craftsmen; of all the crafts fields, fiber work is expanding most rapidly, possibly because up to the past few years it has had the least exposure. There is a new respect for fiber work; appliqué in particular has created public interest and demand because of its varied approaches. Most fiber projects today center on wall decorations and quilts—although many quilts, too, are designed to be hung on walls. Industry and big business are increasingly involved in crafts—many craftsmen now make a good living doing commissioned work in this field, designing and producing one-of-a-kind pieces. Others produce a limited number of certain pieces; many craftsmen are teaching, or are actively engaged in gallery or museum work. The products of fabric artists today are as varied as the artists themselves. These textile craftsmen are using time-tried techniques, but their work is exploding with luxurious and opulent expression—new uses of color, new juxtaposition of design, new mixtures of fabrics and textures, new dimensions in added layers, stuffing, or quilting.

If you are professionally inclined, where you can best market your product depends on what your product is. Craft fairs are raising their standards; no longer do we associate them with the "busy hands at home" syndrome. There is, however, a more discriminating customer class in galleries and museums than at craft fairs; the gallery goer is looking for art more than craft, is usually willing to pay more, and considers work sold through the gallery more selective. Keep in mind that galleries charge for their services—usually around 40 percent.

There are many good craft shops scattered throughout the country; some of these are cooperatives, some are privately owned. If you join a cooperative, you will be expected to do your share of work in the administration or managing of it, and you may have to take your turn at selling, too. Most of the good, privately owned craft shops are very discriminating about the crafts they select for sales; they are aware of their customer's preferences, but they also do a good job of advertising and promoting their stock. Some shops take only on consignment; you run a risk in this case of having your products returned to you unsold, and even a little shopworn. If your work is sold, however, you will get more money on commission than if the shop buys outright, for then you receive only half of its final price. These are all options for you to consider when and if the time comes to take the giant step from amateur to professional status.

You might want to teach fabric art and craft work; a good craftsman is not necessarily a good teacher, but if you have the talent and ability to inspire others, then you could consider this. As a teacher, you have a responsibility to your classes. Be sure you know your subject, have samples of each technique and pattern you expect to teach, and keep the samples fresh, new, and exciting. Don't leave lessons and workshops to chance—*plan* them ahead of time. And be sure you know the answers to questions your students might ask—if you don't know, tell them you'll find out. If you are a good teacher, many in your classes will become repeaters, and they will also tell others about you. Teaching is a challenge, and it is also exciting; and you must always keep a step or two ahead of your classes—when they reach one level, you should already be on the next.

Expose yourself to what's happening in the fiber field; subscribe to a good craft magazine, go to exhibits, and look for new needle images; always keep yourself open to new ideas, new directions, new experiences. Experiment with line and pattern, change shape and form, study the play of light on textures, and don't be afraid to change or break the rules. A good jazz musician improvises on the melody, limited only by his talent, his imagination, and the framework of the tune itself. He touches base, or "comes back home," at the end of the chorus; you have the same freedom to improvise in your work. Many "old-timers" or tradition-bound needleworkers may be disturbed by this, as a classical music lover is often disturbed by jazz, but remember, you can't possibly go anywhere if you are standing still. Whatever you end up doing with appliqué, whether it's a lot or a little, the key word is *enjoy!*

Throughout this book I have presented different techniques and different methods for appliqué, trying to stress that the sky is the limit—ultimately, the choice of design, fabric, and stitches is yours. The result of what you do with these ingredients, and how you do it, is up to you; through trial and experiment, you learn the easiest and best way for you to work. You undoubtedly will change direction as you go along—not once, but many times, perhaps constantly. Life is change, and this is the way we all learn.

The work represented in this book was done by professionals and amateurs alike. For some needleworkers, appliqué is a hobby, a creative outlet; others teach it; still others are professional designers and/or producing craftsmen eager to exhibit and sell their work. Some were educated and trained in art schools; most simply "picked it up," took courses, learned from books, or plunged happily into this creative pool. Ignorance often is bliss, and it often leads to exciting discoveries. If you don't *know* the rules or boundaries, you can't very well break them. If you're unhampered by tradition and known and accepted methods, who knows but you might stumble on something fresh and new? Curiosity leads to uncharted lands.

At any rate, some of the artist-craftsmen who have shared their work have also shared some observations on the way they work, and here are some brief summaries.

THE LAST WORD

GLADYS BOALT

Gladys Boalt studied illustration and advertising at Pratt Institute in New York City. She is a fabric artist-designer and designs appliqué and quilted articles for a specialty shop in New York City. She also has many commissions for quilts and teaches appliqué and quilting.

She does a full-scale detailed drawing of each project, which is color-coded or shaded; it is then transferred to fabric with a light box. She prefers working with all-cotton fabrics, in percale and broadcloth weights, but often resorts to cotton blends to get the right shadings. She also takes full advantage of the bias grain in fabrics, cuts the shapes on the bias, and sews them in place. The bias edge is very easy to turn under, and in most cases Ms. Boalt does not have to clip for curves.

She prefers hand appliqué and uses a size 10 needle, an English egg-eye between. She waxes all her thread to minimize knots and tangling. She is meticulous in her work, and her stitches are so tiny and so uniform that they are almost invisible. She relies on embroidery stitches to bring her work to life and uses one strand of six-strand floss; this is also waxed. Much of her work is with pictures or hangings and quilts. She designed the Putnam County Quilt of New York (see Plate 15) and supervised its making. This may possibly be one of the outstanding masterpiece quilts to come from the Bicentennial year of 1976.

JANIE BURKE

Janie Burke is an art teacher in an elementary school and much of her fabric art is a direct result of her close contact with children—the alphabet spread (page 148) is a good example.

Ms. Burke draws her designs, then experiments with fabrics before making final decisions. She likes all textures—velvets and silks to cottons—and has created her own textile designs for some of her pieces—one with linoleum block printing, and another by drawing her designs in wax with a tjanting on muslin. The muslin was dyed, the designs (animals and letters) cut out, then appliquéd to dyed muslin squares to make a soft book.

MARGARET CUSACK

Margaret Cusack is a professional fabric artist. In recent years she has specialized in fabric portraits and has immortalized many well-known personalities in this medium. Sometimes she sketches her subjects herself; more often, she uses a photographic blowup for a working pattern. From this, she traces pattern pieces on fabric, using a light box. She also uses the light box to trace the entire portrait on background fabric; after the appliqués are positioned on the background, Ms. Cusack sprays the back of the pieces lightly with glue to hold them in place for sewing. She uses polyester batting, or stuffing, to pad certain areas and appliqués entirely with machine, using a closed zigzag stitch. She uses all fabrics, from corduroy to brocade and satin. Much of her work now is commissioned; she submits a paste-up for approval before the final sewing.

Ms. Cusack has exhibited extensively in galleries and craft shops; she worked previously as a graphic designer, set designer, and advertising art director. She won an Emmy Award for television set design in 1971; she now has a shop in Brooklyn, New York, Margaret, Frank and Friends, Inc., where she and several others produce many of her designs in fabric. A recent commission was for three 5' 9" hangings, appliquéd on both sides, on a harvest theme. These appliqués will hang permanently in a new Midwestern building.

She is listed in *Who's Who in American Art 1978*.

CHRIS WOLF EDMONDS

Chris is a young Kansas quilt maker and teacher, as talented as she is pretty. Although she had no formal art training, the combination of design, color, and workmanship lavished on each of her pieces has made her a prize winner several times over. Her George Washington quilt, pictured on page 93, is an example of her meticulous and stunning needlework. She often uses an opaque projector to enlarge a design, then draws it full scale. She then transfers the design to fabric using a light box made from a storm window. Her work is done almost entirely by hand, and her special field is pictorial appliqué. She quilts in an oval hoop, with running stitches that are tiny and remarkably even. Chris is greatly in demand as a teacher and designer throughout the Midwest. She also designed and helped to make the Douglas County, Kansas, Bicentennial Quilt.

ELEANOR LOECHER

Eleanor Loecher is another professional fabric artist who studied art in college and also in postgraduate work. She was especially talented in figure drawing and illustration, and the transition from pencil to needle was easy for her. Most of her time is concentrated on pictures and tapestries featuring faces, or figures in motion.

She works almost solely with printed fabrics, from dress- to upholstery-weight, and she appliqués with an industrial machine, which, as she says, responds to her every whim. She enjoys the play of textures and works fabric against fabric for the most interesting effects. She is always concerned with form and shape in appliqué, and this is evident in the whimsy and vitality of her work. She often fits many small pieces of fabric together to create a shape, and fabric itself suggests a design. She is particularly fond of overall contemporary prints—many times, she has used the same print for a face, or hair, or a building, truly a multifaceted fabric. She "draws" easily and spontaneously with the sewing machine needle and pads her work as she goes.

She puts borders on her pictures, combining two or three printed fabrics for this, then mounts the finished work on canvas stretchers.

Like the rest of us, she is a "fabriholic" and says she has three fire extinguishers' worth in her present stockpile!

SUSIE MONTGOMERY

Susie Montgomery for many years has been exploring the field of appliqué stitchery; her love and mastery of this led her into designing and teaching. Her animal designs are especially captivating; she incorporates into her work a delightful sense of whimsy. She has an excellent color sense and uses embroidery as an integral part of her designs. She especially enjoys working with

Mexican cotton but occasionally substitutes other fabrics such as kettle cloth or Indian-head because of the expense. For a long time she worked directly without a pattern, cutting spontaneously into fabric. She found this to be a wasteful method for her and now works from a pattern—sometimes a detailed drawing, other times a rough sketch that serves as a guide.

MARTHA OPDAHL

Peruvian-born Martha Opdahl has studied textiles, crafts, and techniques of many different cultures and explored their artistic possibilities. Appliqué and stitchery have long been her media, and she is also a proficient quilter; many of her appliqué pieces end up as bed quilts or wall hangings.

Ms. Opdahl is particularly interested in reverse appliqué; her Flower Garden Quilt (see Plate 4 and page 76), a first-prize winner in a nationwide contest in 1977, was made entirely in this technique. She used solid colors throughout the quilt, mixing all shades, and set the quilt together with random-size blocks. Her innovative use of the reverse appliqué technique caused a great deal of criticism, especially among traditionalists, but Ms. Opdahl may have opened up a vast expansion for appliqué lovers.

She prefers to work with all-cotton percales and broadcloths and uses matching thread run over beeswax. She also uses a blind hemming stitch and pins rather than bastes. She works with an oval embroidery hoop; a 9-in. size fits her hand easily, and there is more working area exposed in an oval than in a round hoop. She uses a large frame for full-size quilts but quilts smaller articles without frame or hoop. Recently, experimenting with reverse appliqué, she has used as many as twelve layers of fabric instead of the customary five or six. She divides her stack to eliminate bulk in handling and works with each stack separately before joining them. She cuts a great deal of fabric away and spreads her design over the top layer to the extent that it is no longer a dominant color in the finished design. The cutouts or cutaways from some of the layers are used as patterns for subsequent layers of fabric. This is a demanding medium, but an exciting one.

Ms. Opdahl has exhibited widely and has won many awards for her work.

MARY BELLE OSTLUND

Mary Belle Ostlund made her first appliqué quilt in 1965. She has been making them ever since, and many of her quilts are prize winners. She recently won first prize and best-in-show at a large nationwide quilt exhibit held in Warren, Michigan. She uses both prints and solids in her work and draws her designs completely before she transfers them to fabric. The design for her first quilt came from *Woman's Day* magazine, but since then she has garnered her ideas from illustrations, wallpaper, paper napkins, and greeting cards. She says she is not an artist by any means, but she can adapt ideas and drawings to create her designs. Her work is mostly in a traditional vein, typical, for instance, of the bridal and masterpiece quilts; it is very finely done. She has experimented with using printed fabrics for shading and color gradation, and this gives an unusual depth to her work.

CAROLE PUGLIESE

Carole Pugliese began her career as a stylist for a fabric company. As her knowledge of fabrics grew, she became interested in appliqué work, experimenting with texture, color, and shape in designs. She claims she cannot draw, and most of her designs are adapted or refined from photographs. She also claims she cannot do hand stitching and relies completely on the machine and the zigzag stitch. She was always interested in architecture, especially old houses, both privately or publicly owned. This interest sparked her present career, for Ms. Pugliese makes fabric and lace portraits of houses. The lace element was almost an afterthought—at least, it was a happy accident. Ms. Pugliese found a wealth of old laces and embroideries at a tag sale and promptly began to incorporate them into her work. "They were," she said, "crying to be used."

She does a very rough draft of the picture content—perhaps the house with plants and lawn, or perhaps just a doorway or a special feature of a building. She uses all and any fabrics for both background and building, but it is her unique use of lace that distinguishes her pictures. She works on the floor, where her background material is spread out. She works mostly from photos, then cuts shapes directly into fabric and moves them around until she is satisfied with their placement, trimming surplus fabric as needed. She does not baste. When the shapes are pinned in place, she begins to stitch them down; she often makes changes as she goes along, and the finished pictures are framed or stretched.

SOME BASIC CONVERSIONS

⅛ inch (in.)	3 millimeters (mm)
¼ in.	6 mm
½ in.	1.3 centimeters (cm)
1 in.	2.5 cm
2 in.	5 cm
3 in.	7.5 cm
4 in.	10 cm
5 in.	12.5 cm
6 in.	15 cm
12 in.	30.5 cm
24 in.	61 cm
36 in.	91.5 cm
45 in.	114.5 cm
50 in.	127 cm
1 yard (yd.)	0.95 meters (m)
2 yd.	1.85 m
3 yd.	2.75 m
4 yd.	3.80 m
5 yd.	4.60 m
6 yd.	5.50 m

FABRIC WIDTH CONVERSION

35/36 in.	65 cm
39 in.	100 cm
44/45 in.	115 cm
50 in.	127 cm
72 in.	180 cm